50{

LAST OF THE HARD HAT DIVERS

LAST OF THE HARD HAT DIVERS

Bob Sinclair

Book Guild Publishing
Sussex, England

First published in Great Britain in 2010 by
The Book Guild Ltd
Pavilion View
19 New Road
Brighton, BN1 1UF

Typeset in Baskerville by
Ellipsis Books Limited, Glasgow

Printed in Great Britain by
CPI Antony Rowe

A catalogue record for this book is available from
The British Library.

ISBN 978 1 84624 435 3

Prologue

Originally this book was intended solely to be a collection of a young boy's memories of his own, and his family's, experiences prior to, and inclusive of, the years of World War 2. However, after I had recounted one of my diving stories, a chance remark by my youngest daughter Pamela altered the whole prospectus. She said, 'Dad, I never heard that before, you should write that story in your book.'

What followed the war years became a part autobiographical account of my life as a hard hat diver. The characters within these pages are, or were, real people with whom I shared the tiniest drip in the great infinite ocean of Time. With them I experienced the whole gamut of human emotions: humour and pathos, both thrilling and tragic, and the oh-so-near misses of an early entry into eternity beneath the greeny blue of the sea. Today I still feel proud to be one of The Last of the Hard Hat Divers.

This book
is
dedicated to my darling wife
Mabe

Contents

1

The Hard Hat Men

David Bell	Liverpool	Deceased
Martin Bendicks	Leith	Deceased
Ian Crow	Leith	(Unknown)
Leslie Doe	Australia	(Unknown)
George Donaldson	Leith	Deceased
Tom Eadie	Dundee	Deceased
Steven Fox	Edinburgh	Deceased
Alexander Green	Dundee	Deceased
Geoffrey Kane	England	(Unknown)
Alexander McGill	Leith	Deceased
Tom Murphy	Leith	Deceased
Jack Sayers	England	(Unknown)
Bob Sinclair	Edinburgh	Author
Anthony Sparrow	England	Deceased
Samuel Stanley	HMS *Vernon*	Deceased
Peter Taylor	Liverpool	Deceased
James Ward	Edinburgh	Deceased

2

Divers Only Have Daughters

I knew the police pathologist had something on his mind, as he was studying me closely. I also knew it would have nothing to do with the sheriff's enquiry. We had been advised not to discuss the case, while waiting to give our evidence. One-eyed Fergie was restlessly pacing up and down the waiting-room floor; it appeared he was uncomfortable being in an Edinburgh court-house, even as a witness. We had been told that a murder trial had taken over our courtroom time slot but, since then, the passage of time appeared to slow down all the more. Two or three times I caught my own mind trying to alleviate the boredom by slipping off into a daydream of bygone days.

Each time the pathologist's eyes pulled me back into that small waiting room. His relaxed attitude suggested he was used with the vagaries of the justiciary. He puffed on his pipe, as he watched me. At last he spoke.

'Have you heard, diver, that something seems to happen to the Y chromosome when a man has been diving for a while, so divers only have daughters?'

'Yes I've heard that, in fact while I was in the Royal Navy in 1953 they ran a survey which showed as high as eighty-five per cent of children fathered by divers were girls. Ten per cent were boys and five per cent had no children at all.'

Obviously the pathologist was not a man to hurry a conversation. He nodded his head and sat there, blowing smoke into the air. One-eyed Fergie had taken an interest in what was being discussed and sat down to listen.

'Yes' the pathologist eventually agreed, 'I read that.' And once more he seemed to go off in a reverie of his own thoughts. One-eyed Fergie was showing obvious signs of impatience as he looked at us both in turn, possibly wondering who would speak first. The pathologist removed his pipe and wiped his lips with his free hand.

'Did you know they ran the same survey in the diving departments of the much bigger American Navy with surprisingly similar results?'

'No,' I admitted, 'I did not know that.'

Now there was a real pause and one-eyed Fergie lost interest, rose and began his pacing up and down again. The pathologist stroked his chin with the stem of his pipe but his eyes remained focused on mine. Eventually he asked, 'What do you think of that?'

'A load of rubbish,' I answered, and the clock on the wall ticked on, and on.

'Really?' he said incredulously, eyebrows raised. 'Yes really,' I answered, and the clock ticked on once more.

'Have you a family yourself?'

'I have,' I said simply, thinking, I will play him at his own game, a short answer followed by a long pause.

It worked, for he asked almost immediately, 'What do you have?'

'I have five daughters,' I answered.

Both he and One-eyed Fergie had the good grace to laugh heartily at my stupid sense of humour. 'No boys then,' the pathologist remarked.

'I did stop diving for three years after the birth of my third daughter and my wife miscarried a wee boy. I then resumed diving full time and we had another two daughters.'

The pathologist nodded and, clenching his teeth firmly on the pipe stem, he continued puffing away contentedly. One-eyed Fergie had stopped his pacing up and down and was again showing interest in the conversation.

'Seriously though,' I said, 'there seems to be something happens to the Y chromosome where divers and Tunnel Tigers are concerned.'

One-eyed Fergie sat down again and asked, 'How do you know?'

'Well,' I said, 'I suppose there will always be an element of doubt, but my present diving buddy, Martin Bendicks, has no family at all and has been diving continuously since the 1940s. My previous buddy, Sandy McGill, also started diving then and when he married, his wife and he had no children for years and years. Then out of the blue their son Dennis was born. Sandy and Peggy got an even bigger shock, seventeen years later when their second son Neil was born.'

The pathologist knocked his pipe out into an ashtray. 'I suppose the scientists will find the answer in years to come,' he said.

An usher put a stop to the conversation by calling out loudly and One-eyed Fergie left us to give his evidence before the sheriff. We sat in silence for some time until I was called to give my own evidence.

On the particular day of the tragedy, while employed as a diver by the Leith Docks Commission, I was renewing the rubber seals on the gates of the Alexandra dry dock, in Leith Docks, when my linesman George Smiles came on the diver phone and told me I had to come up immediately. He explained that a sailor had fallen overboard from his ship in the Imperial Dock and had vanished beneath the surface. We were told to make all possible speed to get there and try to find him. I had George remove my helmet and front and back weights but kept on my boots and corselet. A hard hat diver is supposed to strip right down before the boat gets underway but I felt speed was paramount on this occasion.

We arrived at the ship, lying alongside No. 7 Imperial Dock berth to find both an ambulance and a fire engine were already there. A sizeable crowd thronged the quayside all around. We were told a simple staging had been lowered from the deck and some Spanish seamen had been set to work painting the ship's side earlier that morning. While climbing back on board for dinner, one of the men, Angel Gonzales Gonzales, twenty-six, had fallen over the side and since none of the sailors could swim they had watched the unfortunate man struggling in the water. One of the dockers on board was One-eyed Fergie, a first-class swimmer. He was working on the after-hold when he heard the commotion. He ran along the deck and saw a pair of red gloves waving above the surface. He jumped on the ship's gunnel and dived over the side, only to surface and find the sailor had gone down. He swam round underwater for a time, before having to give up, exhausted. He showed George the exact spot he had last seen the seaman on the surface. George dropped a shot line where Fergie indicated, with a search line attached to it, and returning on board the diving boat he made the other end of the shot line fast to the diving ladder. As he replaced my weights and helmet, I remember thinking, this could be a long haul of a search. The visibility on the bottom was about two feet and as soon as I started to swing on the search line the silt of centuries boiled up around me and left visibility virtually nil. I had travelled about twenty feet on my very first circle of the search line, when out of the gloom came a pair of bright red gloves, which actually landed right on my front light. It was almost unbelievable, I had him within minutes of hitting the bottom. Of course time was immaterial, he had been underwater for the best part of an hour.

'Take up my lines George,' I said over the phone. 'I have him and I'll spindle up with him.'

Holding the poor young Spaniard under my left arm, I depressed my spindle valve, shutting off my exhaust air and thereby inflating my suit. I left the bottom with a rush, calling as I did so, 'Take up the slack George and take me away!'

As soon as I bounced to the surface George towed me slowly over to the stone steps of the quay. I duly delivered the drowned man to the waiting ambulance men and this was the evidence I gave at the sheriff's enquiry.

It was with the utmost sadness that I thought of a young sailor, a man who had been sailing on the high seas for years, drowning in the calm waters of dockland, with a blue sky overhead and a summer sun shining brightly on the warm waters of the harbour. It came down to the fact that not one of the Spanish crew on board that ship could swim. I sat for two whole days in that waiting room, before being called before the sheriff. I found during that time that I began thinking back over my own early life.

I was born on the sixteenth of February 1931 and my father took me to the swimming baths almost every day after my birth. As soon as the sea heated up a bit, he also took me to the beach and into the sea. As a direct result of this, I was swimming both underwater and on the surface before I had learned to walk. At six years old, my father took me to the once famous Leith Sands, where horse-racing was regularly staged in bygone days. We swam out and around the Martello Tower, the people of Leith called it the 'Tally Toor'. It was a fortress built during the Napoleonic

Wars and for a while it served as a prison, holding captured Frenchmen. To this present time it is still possible to read the inscriptions these poor devils carved on the inside of its walls.

Such a simple thing, to teach young people to swim, to become accustomed to shallow water to begin with, and once confident in the water, to do the doggie paddle and swim. I also had time to reflect on the many times I myself had cheated death in near-fatal diving accidents over the years. Those that my wife Mabel knew nothing about until I retired from the diving and that earliest wartime incident, where I could easily have become one of the first casualties of the war.

My mind wandered back to that time, almost forty years ago. The time of the run rabbit, run rabbit, run run run.

3

Run Rabbit, Run Rabbit

In the year 1938, my father, Arthur Sinclair, was a seaman aboard a ship delivering scrap metal to Germany, via the port of Hamburg. He and one of his shipmates went ashore one night to have a drink in one of the local bars close by the docks. There were very few customers present and the boss of the bar, who appeared to be a bit of a genial giant, asked if the two seamen would like to challenge him and his son to a few games of snooker. Both the owner and his son spoke reasonably good English, albeit in a pidgin English style. The younger German began setting up the snooker table, so the two seamen agreed to play.

'You Engleesh sailors, ja?' the boss asked.

'No,' Dad answered, 'we are Scottish sailors.'

'But you on Engleesh ship ja?'

'Yes our ship is English right enough,' Dad agreed.

'What you bring us for Germany?' the boss asked, chalking his cue and preparing to break-off.

'Just a lot of old scrap iron, nothing special,' said Dad.

The boss and his son appeared to be good company at first, so the sailors had accepted a best of seven frames tournament. The first two frames were closely contested, but both went to the seafarers.

'You haff great luck,' said the boss. 'Our luck must change soon.'

'Yes' said my dad, agreeing with him. 'It sometimes works out that way, Lady Luck swings one way for a while, then it can equal out later on.'

Just then the younger German missed a fairly simple red and my dad prepared to take his shot. The boss chided his son, in what seemed to be a jocular manner. 'You not prepare properly before you play,' he said, but his smile was more like a grimace. 'There is no luck, if you prepare properly.'

As they played on, the Germans' good nature evaporated rapidly, especially after they lost the third frame as well. Upon the seamen winning the fourth and final frame, the boss of the bar became openly hostile towards them. The sailors decided to leave and they finished their drinks. As they did so the older German snarled, 'So, you beat us ja! But ve soon prepare properly, and bye and bye ve beat you and ve give you back all the scrap you bring here.'

Before leaving Germany that same year, my father witnessed a military march-past of goose-stepping German soldiers. This was followed by a show of army strength, with bren-gun carriers, armoured vehicles of all kinds and finally, row after row of seemingly endless tanks.

Arriving home to 21 Craigentinny Road, Edinburgh, my father invited some of my aunts and uncles over for a game of cards on a Saturday night, which was their usual entertainment in those days. I was only a little boy at that time and I was left to play with my toys, quite happily, on the carpet in front of the fire. I was not aware of the fact that my brain was recording the conversations taking place among the adult members of my family. Later on in life I found to my own amazement that I had the power to recall specific days and even what was said, and by whom, on those days. I would eventually discover this ability appeared to be handed down to me via the gene pool, since my father and his father before him had similar abilities. As the adults played, they discussed the situation that was developing on the Continent. Uncle Alex produced a copy of a newspaper which had a large photograph across its front page showing massed tanks rolling past a saluting Hitler. Under the photograph was a headline which read, 'Among these cardboard cut-outs, can you spot the real tank?'

'Do they expect us to believe that they have as many tanks as that lot?' Uncle Alex said with a derisive laugh as he slapped the newspaper with one hand. My dad looked up from his hand of cards. 'They are all real,' he said with some vehemence. 'I can assure you, they are all real and Hitler is looking for revenge for what we did to Germany last time.'

'Do you think he might have a go at us Attie?' asked Uncle Walter.

Dad tossed his cards face down on the table. 'Believe me Wattie, I'm so sure of it, I'm going to send Mary and the bairns up to Shetland for their safety, while I'm away at sea.'

'Oh Attie, do you really think there is going to be another war?' my Auntie Ruby asked.

'I'm sure of it' my dad answered. 'I have already written to my brother Tommy, asking him to find a croft house, somewhere up in North Roe or around Hillswick. I would not even consider Lerwick to be safe at this time.'

So our extended family, myself aged seven, sister Isobel aged three, our mother Mary with her sisters Ruby and Charlotte and their mother, our Grandma Thomson, all travelled up to Shetland on the ferry boat, *St Sunniva*. Arriving in Lerwick, we then took a bus approximately thirty miles north to the little village of Mossbank, where we were to live in an empty croft house belonging to my mother's aunt, Jeannie Thomson, who had her own house in Hillswick.

I remember so well that first night in the small house. We youngsters were deemed tired, after the long journey, so we were put to bed in the living room. I lay awake listening to the conversation of my elders. The room was very dimly lit by a small pump-up paraffin lamp that hung from the low ceiling.

'So,' my mother said, 'Mum can sleep in the far bedroom by herself and both of you will have to sleep together in the other bedroom. I will sleep with the bairns tonight and we will sort it all out in the morning.'

Aunt Ruby began to argue. 'I thought Jeannie said there were another two rooms in the attic, why can't we go up there?'

'So there is,' Mum answered, 'but this house has not been lived in for a while, you can go up there if you want.'

'What do you mean?' Ruby said in sudden alarm. 'You don't think there might be mice up there do you?'

Ah! I was born to be a torment of a boy. I remembered Aunt Ruby's great fear of mice and pretending to be fast asleep, I slid one arm under my pillow and began scratching faintly on the wall.

'Oh! Listen,' said Ruby, 'that sounds like a mouse.' I naturally stopped scratching, while they listened together in silence.

'Even if it is a mouse it's not going to hurt you,' my Aunt Chattie said quietly.

'I hate the beastly things,' Ruby answered loudly. My cue to resume scratching.

'Och Ruby' said Mum, 'I don't like them either but they're probably more scared of us than we are of them.'

'I can't stay here,' Ruby said desperately.

'Don't be silly Ruby,' said Grandma Thomson. 'We're out in the middle of the country and it's dark; where would you go?'

'Listen again for a moment,' said Chattie, 'I think they might just be in the attic.' She was trying to calm Ruby down. Of course, as soon as they stopped talking, I stopped scratching. I played my little game for quite a while and had them in a fine state, before I tired of it and fell asleep. It backfired on me, however, because from that night onwards I was the only one who slept in the attic.

For quite some time I did not go to school and was more or less allowed to please myself, playing around the croft or down on the seashore.

My aunt Charlotte, or 'Chattie' as everybody called her, was the youngest of my mother's sisters and the most recently married. Uncle George Selvester came to stay with us for a while to be beside his young wife, just before the war began. He promised he would take me fishing off the Craigs – this was what the Shetland people called the flat-topped rocks on the seashore which just managed to stay above the surface when the tide was at its highest. I remember how disappointed I was when he gave me a small garden cane, with a piece of string about four feet long tied to one end and a hook tied to the other end. Even at the tender age of seven, I still knew this was no use.

We set off and were soon on the Craigs. My uncle carried an eighteen-foot long piltock wand, which was a one piece bamboo rod tapered from butt to tip, through natural growth, with eighteen feet of line whipped onto its tip. It had no reel but when upright the end of the line was easily held in one hand. Six haddock hooks hung on short droppers at the line's end. These hooks had the pink bristles of a boar pig tied on them, in the form of trout flies. My uncle swung the long wand and the makeshift flies landed thirty-six feet away. He slowly lifted the wand, bringing the hooks skating in on the surface towards us and lo!, each hook soon had a plump golden-sided pollack fish firmly embedded on it. My little cane could hardly reach the water at my feet, so naturally, nothing came near it.

I stood there, thoroughly miserable, watching my uncle filling the large basket we had brought with us. This was not just sport to us, it was producing food for the whole family and the nearest neighbours, for Shetland people always shared their catch.

An old man came striding along the Craigs towards us. He was obviously very angry. He shouted at my uncle in a broad Shetland accent. 'Man' he roared, 'what's dis du is doing to the peerie boy? Dat's a load o dirt the lad's face wid tell dee he kens he will get naethin' wi a peerie cane like yon.'

'He's quite happy,' my uncle said lamely. The old man took the cane out of my hands and threw it onto the rocks behind us. 'Happy my fit,' he said in a quieter voice, and turned to me. 'Jist du wait here an I will geng and fetch dee a proper wand.'

The old man was as good as his word and a short while later he returned with a bamboo wand which was nine feet long, ideal for a young boy. Now I could cast out eighteen feet. I caught mainly silocks, the Shetland name for the younger, smaller fish, and Uncle George was catching piltocks, the more adult fish. It mattered not, I was catching fish.

My idyllic life came to an abrupt halt when my mother arranged for me to be taken to school by an older cousin, who lived nearby, although this cousin, Betty Thomson, was only ten years old at the time. She appeared to be well grown up to me. On that first morning I was given a tin can with some dry cocoa and sugar in it. I was also given two turves of peat to carry under my arm to give to the teacher. Betty also had two turves of peat and carried a bag of sandwiches for our lunch. She took me by the hand and we set off. Although well wrapped up, I remember how cold that first journey was, trudging through a few inches of snow, with a northerly breeze blowing in our faces.

The school we were to attend was more than a mile and a

half from our houses. When we eventually arrived we found the schoolmistress lighting a black cast iron stove in a little ante-room, next to the single classroom, that formed the whole school. I gave her the two turves of peat, which were the fuel for the stove. We were a small class of eight pupils, so the teacher had sixteen turves of peat to heat the school and boil the huge kettle for our cocoa at dinner time. It was a cold, cold winter, that of 1938–1939 and spring and summer brought a welcome relief from the cold. Then came the day the little blaeberries formed on the heather-clad hills. Gran Thomson decided to make some home-made jam. She soon organised a berry-picking party of herself, my mother Mary, her sisters Charlotte and Ruby, Isobel and myself. The sun shone out of a clear blue sky and we were soon all hard at work picking berries on the slopes of a fairly steep hill. In the distance we heard the drone of an aeroplane, slowly becoming louder and louder. It had a strange 'Whoo-whoo-whoo' sound, an inter-mittent beat, one which we would all get to know so well throughout the war.

Over the crest of the hill, with a sudden violent increase in volume, came an aeroplane, barely twenty feet above the hilltop, and it passed directly over us. We saw the pilot clearly, his cockpit cover was fully back and he leaned to one side and stared down at us, through a pair of heavy looking black goggles, his chin-strap hung loosely from his helmet. He banked and, turning in a slow circle, came back over us again. He seemed to be studying us closely.

'Oh Mary,' said Gran, 'I think that's a German plane.'

Aunt Chattie began waving to the pilot and smiling up at him at the same time. Ruby said, 'Why are you waving to him, if he's a German?' Her voice was loaded with criticism.

'You should wave too,' Chattie said, still smiling broadly. 'If he's a German, we should appear friendly.' Our mum now started waving as well. 'Chattie is right,' she said, and she too smiled up at the pilot. 'Let's all wave to him.'

So we did, all except Granny Thomson, who it seemed could no longer bear to even look up at the plane. We could see the thick black crosses, one on each wing. The pilot turned away and we watched him gaining height as he flew towards the north. He was little more than a speck in the blue sky when a sudden loud crump 'crump' suggested to us he had dropped bombs on an empty hillside far away to the north.

When the story was reported in the newspapers, Dad gave us an immediate recall back home to Edinburgh. That pilot was responsible for the very first wartime casualty in Britain. He spared us, but he killed a rabbit on that lonely northerly hillside. Hence the song, 'Run rabbit, run rabbit, run run run' took on the mantle of a derisive song against the Germans.

Down in London the comedy duo Flanagan and Allen dubbed in different words and sang the parody in the theatres, to the amusement of the audiences. At that time they could not possibly foresee the terrible carnage that was to come to our cities and civilians, once pilots inured themselves to the killing. We were fortunate to meet our pilot so early on in the war.

We did not return home immediately, but stayed temporarily with my grandfather, Robert Sinclair, the man I myself was named after. His house at number 12, Commercial Street, had its foundations actually set in the waters of Lerwick harbour. Below the living accommodation of this large stone-built building and well beneath the road level was a large boat shed, where Granddad kept his Shetland model boat during the winter months. A set of stone steps to one side of the house gave access down from street level to a large open yard, adjacent to the boat shed, which culminated in a pier running out past the house, allowing fishing boats to tie up and purchase fuel oil from the old man.

Three large circular tanks sat on chocks in the yard. Pipelines ran from the tanks and connected with delivery hoses, which ran out along the top of the pier. This, then, was how my old granddad made his living, still trading, although he was sixty-eight years old at the time. It was in Granddad's shed I first became aware of the influence of the sense of smell and taste on a very young boy's memory. I was allowed to play in his boat when it lay in the shed, with mast and sails fully erected. I sat in the boat and smelled tarry rope and the pungent smell of salt fishing lines and fresh paint.

Sitting there, I became aware of the taste of Shetland bannocks suddenly flooding my mouth and instantly bringing back an earlier memory of about three years previously, when I had played in the same boat at five years of age. Ever since that day my sense of taste and smell have triggered many memories of my earlier life.

We arrived home to Edinburgh to find many changes had taken place. Firstly my father had built an Anderson shelter in the back garden. Sunk deep in the earth, it had a narrow bunk bed on either side and a central seating bench. A short set of wooden steps gave access down into it. When first we looked inside it there was about six inches of water in its bottom and no matter how often it was baled out, it came back again surprisingly quickly.

The front, side and back gardens were devoid of flowers – instead, a large crop of potatoes took up all the growing space, and the heavy shaws looked very healthy indeed. Dad was not home, having recently joined Christian Salvesen's oil tanker the SS *Coronda*, as her boatswain, or bosun as it is normally called. In Craigentinny golf course, adjacent to our back garden, four concrete emplacements had been erected. Each one had circular rails on its top and on the rails sat four huge anti-aircraft guns. A small camp of Nissen huts had also been built close to the guns, to house the soldiers who manned them.

From that time onwards we would waken at night to the wail of the air-raid sirens, followed by Grandma Thomson, who lived in the top flat, calling through the letterbox, 'Mary, Mary, hurry get the bairns up, we have to get them to the shelter.' That dear old lady must have flown down four flights of stairs in her anxiety to see us safely in the shelter. Dressed in our pyjamas and wrapped in a blanket we would be rushed out into the freezing cold of the black, dark night. Once safely inside the shelter with the blackout curtain in place, Gran and our mother would light little candles, which were kept in a box in the shelter. We would lie there, in the flickering candlelight and watch the beads of condensation trickling down the corrugated walls. We would listen intently for the by now familiar sound of the engine we first heard in the wilds of Shetland.

We often heard the planes in the distance and the 'crump crump' of far off bombs. Sometimes the planes would come our way and as the engine noise grew louder, our guns would open up in a deafening crescendo, which terrified our little family. One night, on the sixth of August 1941, we were sound asleep, no siren woke us, no engine noise, no fretting Grandma, no shelter, then suddenly there came an explosion of such intensity, a tremendous noise accompanied by a violent shaking of our house. We all leapt out of our beds. Gran duly appeared, wide-eyed. She said, 'Oh Mary, that must have been awfully close to us, should we not go out to the shelter?'

'No Mum,' our mother said. 'We're staying here. God knows what that was but I just cannot bring myself to go outside tonight.'

In the morning I went out and met some of my friends who

were all talking about the explosion. Almost opposite our school stood the medieval Craigentinny Castle, about 100 yards up the road from our house. When we walked up the road we saw that half the east wall of the castle was gone. A wall built hundreds of years ago and consisting of large natural boulders, capable of resisting cannon fire for a considerable time, and yet, in a second it had vanished. A nearby tenement had been cut clean in half. We could see right inside each of the three flats. The middle flat had a piano balanced precariously on the vertical edge of the remaining part of the building. From the roof to the ground it had the appearance of having been cut cleanly down by some huge knife. Our attention turned to some of the lads who were calling us to come back down the road and see something really unusual. We walked halfway back towards our own houses and up a lane which revealed all the back gardens of the houses on either side. There we saw an Anderson shelter, which had been punched down into the ground by an enormous boulder, which was embedded on top of it. This was obviously part of the ancient east wall of the castle. It must have weighed close to two tons, at least, and it had travelled approximately 150 yards from the castle, passing over a row of houses as it did so and landed squarely on the shelter. Had anyone been inside? They could not possibly have survived the shockwave.

I was to learn many years later that the shelter belonged to the Palmer family. If the sirens had gone off that night, my present-day wife Mabel would surely have perished in that shelter. Not only that, but her father, Robert Palmer, had left the castle club barely a half an hour before the bombs fell. The castle club was a long, single storey wooden hut that lay along the inside of the castle's east wall. Here the members could play darts, dominoes and snooker. There was nothing left of the club or the east wall of the castle except rubble and small debris.

*

19

I came to, and realised I had been day-dreaming after all. I was still sitting in the waiting room of the courthouse. It was day one of the trial and the police pathologist was reading a magazine. One-eyed Fergie was shuffling through the remaining magazines on a small table in the middle of the room. I found my thoughts turning inwards once more. It seemed relatively miraculous that my extended family had escaped unscathed during the war. It was true that Uncle George Selvester had been wounded at El Alamein. Uncle Geordie survived four and a half years in a German prisoner of war camp. Uncle Wattie was in the thick of the battle of Monte Casino in Italy. Uncle Alex had a few near things as a petty officer in the Navy and Buncer, my Uncle Peter, survived Convoy 42 and its disastrous voyage to try and help the Russians. My own father probably had the closest call of all, when I began thinking back over the story of the SS *Coronda* and later on 'the captain's bomb'.

4

SS Coronda

The *Coronda* was built in 1899 as a cargo ship by Swan Hunter of Newcastle. She was originally named the SS *Politician* (long before a ship of the same name inspired the story *Whisky Galore*). She belonged to the Charente Steam Ship Co. Ltd of Liverpool. In 1922 she was purchased by Salvesen of Leith, converted into a tanker to carry whale oil and renamed *Coronda*. She spent many years carrying stores to the whaling station of Leith harbour, South Georgia, and returning home to the UK with whale oil. In early 1939 she returned to the UK and my father signed on as her bosun. He had often served in Salvesen's ships in the past, in fact his first trip to South Georgia was in 1920, when he was only eighteen years old.

The SS *Coronda* sailed into the Gare loch on the west coast of Scotland early in the year 1939. She was to remain there for quite some time, for a partial refit, so Dad took the opportunity to book my mother, sister and myself into a hotel in Helensburgh, over one weekend. On the Saturday morning he took me out onto the sand in the centre of the Gare loch and there I saw the *Coronda* for the first time, lying at anchor in the middle of the loch. The 5,000-ton tanker with her four masts made a big impression on me, but as an eight-year-old boy I was more interested in the fact that my dad had promised to let me fish the sea loch.

He showed me how to search for cockles along the line of the ebbing tide. We soon had a good number in the metal pail that Dad carried and he taught me how to interlock the knobbly ends of two cockles and by twisting sideways to open both and remove the baits from inside. I was so excited at the prospect of going fishing I barely felt the cold Scots mist that was slowly soaking us and at the same time half hiding the ship from our view. A little dinghy lay on its side, its painter tied to a large stone. It was high and dry, left behind, halfway down the beach by the ebbing tide. Dad untied the stone and dragged the small boat down into the water and wearing sea boots he soon had it floating. He lifted me on board and we set off, Dad rowing strongly out to the large ship.

We came alongside a companionway, which Dad tied the little boat to and to my dismay he wanted to take me on board to show me around the ship.

'Don't worry,' he said, 'You will have plenty of time for fishing later.'

The climb to the main deck seemed to go on forever but once on board a young boy's wonderment took over and I began to enjoy the experience. As I write this, the powerful smell of red lead paint again fills my nostrils; the seamen appeared to be painting everything in sight. Unlike modern tankers which have their engine room and main accommodation at their stern, the *Coronda* accommodation was almost amidships and the engine room lay immediately behind it. Dad took me down there and showed me the huge steam engine which normally drove the ship. At present it lay silent; only the auxiliary engines were running to provide lighting and power on deck.

Dad walked me through a tunnel which carried the main

drive-shaft from the engine to the stern. He showed me the chocks that supported the shaft and the bearings on each chock, which had to be lubricated by the greasers to prevent overheating. When we reached the stern, I felt a bit afraid, for a Jacobs vertical ladder had to be climbed all the way up to the aft end of the ship. This was an emergency escape ladder. I need not have worried, Dad's strong arms encircled my small body as soon as we started up the iron ladder. It was a long climb up into the ship's stern. I thought I would now be allowed to fish from the small dinghy but this was not to be.

He then took me all the way to the forecastle and into the seamen's mess and sleeping quarters. I met some of the crew, who were having afternoon tea and sandwiches. I was given a mug of strong-tasting tea and Dad put condensed milk in it. He said, 'Help yourself to sugar.' A large bowl of sugar lay on the mess table. There were also two very large tins, one half full of Irish butter, the other half full of strawberry jam. Dad took hold of a loaf of bread and cut off two thick slices. He placed them on a plate in front of me. 'Take as much butter and jam as you want.' The jam was delicious but the butter smelled and tasted rancid.

The weekend was over all too soon. I did do a bit of fishing on the Sunday, catching small cod and flounders, while I was tied securely to the thwart of the dinghy, but once again we returned to Edinburgh, with its constant air-raid sirens and the miserable nights spent in that cold and damp shelter. Then one night my mother began crying hysterically. It seemed that she had been listening to the English traitor William Joyce, known as Lord Haw-Haw, who used to broadcast on the radio from Germany. He had said it was a waste of time waiting for your menfolk to come home, if they were sailors aboard Salvesen's *Coronda*, which had just been sunk by the Luftwaffe. The next day a telegram arrived to say Dad was safe and well. Hereafter, let Dad take up the story.

When we left the Gare loch we sailed to Iceland and took aboard a cargo of fish oil. The last part of our refit had included the installation of a four-point-two Browning Gun on our stern, the idea being to give us some form of defence, should a U-boat try to sink us by gunfire instead of a more costly torpedo. We also took on board a Royal Naval gunner to man it. The first mate of our ship was a man called Robert Sinclair, the same name as both my own father and my wee boy Bobby, anyway, the mate sent for me and said he wanted me to give up my cabin near the stern of the ship to the gunner, so he would be nearer his gun. I duly moved to a cabin just aft of the main accommodation.

On our return journey, I was off watch and asleep in my bunk, when I was suddenly blown out of it and slammed against the opposite bulkhead. A second explosion came as I lay there stunned. I dashed out on deck to find the top of the engine room casing had been blown wide open by the first bomb. The second bomb had seemingly descended into the engine room itself, destroying all the access companionway ladders, and leaving the greasers and engineers trapped down below. Their only chance to get out was through the shaft tunnel and up the aft end emergency escape ladder. It is a strange thing, the fickle finger of fate – the long pause between the second and third bomb gave my shipmates just enough time to race through the tunnel and climb up into the aftercastle, which was then blown sky high, turned around and landed back facing the wrong way. Twenty-one of my shipmates died instantly in the carnage. Incidentally, the naval gunner survived. He had just finished his watch and walked forward to the ship's galley, and there he was sitting, sipping a cup of coffee when the bombing began. There was not the slightest trace left of the cabin I had given over to him, before leaving Iceland. Somebody up above was looking after me. The ship was on fire and taking water aft, the flames were raging across the well deck and black smoke was billowing out of the ruptured engine-room casing.

Captain Sinclair Begg's voice came over a loudhailer: 'Abandon ship! Abandon ship! All hands to boat stations, abandon ship!'

We quickly lowered the lifeboats and rowed away from the stricken ship. We lay well clear of her, for fear that, being an oil tanker, she might explode. We rose and fell to the motion of a lazy swell, but other than that the weather was quite benign for that time of the year.

In the distance we could see Royal Naval ships patrolling around a large outbound convoy. Their guns were firing at the planes that had attacked us. There was no chance they would leave their charges to come to our aid, yet their presence was reassuring. We knew they would report what had happened and no doubt help would arrive in due course.

After a considerable time, our first mate Bob Sinclair stood up in the boat and looking towards our ship he said, 'There is very little change in her freeboard. She is not going to sink suddenly. I want volunteers to go back aboard and fight the fires. I honestly think we might have a chance of saving her.'

To a man, the crew agreed to make the attempt, so we climbed back on board and gathering all the firefighting equipment we could find, we set to the task. It was a horrendous job. The blistering heat was almost unbearable and the well deck was strewn with the burnt-out body parts of our shipmates. One blackened torso was stuck to a spare boom above our heads. The Liverpool and Glasgow Salvage Company arrived on the scene and their firefighting tugboats began to make a difference to the intensity of the flames. Meanwhile, their deep-sea tugs had made their tow ropes fast to our bows and soon had us in tow. It was a race against time; the ship was slowly sinking and fuel oil was spilling from her tanks and thereby being replaced by the sea itself.

It took three full days before the tugs rounded the Isle of Bute and made for Port Bannatyne bay, a sheltered sandy bay on the east coast of the island. With her decks almost awash she was driven ashore on the north side of the bay and there she sat, polluting the sandy beach with her oil.

When the authorities had concluded their gruesome work, only one member of the crew was left unaccounted for. The others were buried in the little churchyard that lies midway between Port Bannatyne and the famous sandy beach of Ettrick Bay, on the west side of the island. After this was completed Mr Thomas, the salvage supervisor, asked for a volunteer from us, the surviving crew members, to accept the job of watchman to guard the ship on a full-time basis at night, while during the day the salvage company would use her as a store ship. I volunteered and was asked by one of my shipmates if I would not be afraid, alone in the ship at night. I replied why should I be afraid, after all it was my shipmates that had died. They would not wish me any harm.

This then, was the start of my employment with the Liverpool and Glasgow Salvage Company. The ship sat on the sandy bottom in a fairly upright position, so living aboard her on my own was no great hardship. On her seaward side, the companionway had been lowered into the water and I had the ship's dinghy moored there permanently. After the day's work was completed, I was able to climb into the boat and row across the bay to Port Bannatyne, and have a drink and a meal in one of the inns or hotels. Invariably I would leave the dinghy in the care of one of the local lads who always seemed to appear on the stone quay as I tied her up. I soon found out that watchmen from some of the other wrecks did the same thing as I did. The local youngsters were only too eager to earn some money by looking after our rowing boats.

One-eyed Fergie dropped his magazine accidentally with a crash, which instantly brought me out of my daydream of the past. It was day two in the waiting room of the Edinburgh courthouse. I sat there thinking how lucky my father had been to change cabins with the Royal Naval gunner aboard the *Coronda*. He had no control over the events that had taken place on that particular day but I found my thoughts turning back to the near-miraculous escape he had had, while being manipulated by his employers, in the case of the 'Captain's bomb'; but first came the story he told us of the *Volundam*.

5

SS Volundam

Not long after we knew Dad was safe, he sent Mum a letter to say he wanted us to come over to the west coast to be nearer to him. We were to come back to the mouth of the Gare loch, to the village of Rhu, where Dad had rented apartments on the seafront, overlooking the River Clyde. We lived there for six glorious weeks during which my sister and I did not go to school at all. Instead, for me, it was all fishing or playing on the seashore again. During this time Dad was offered a permanent job with the salvage company as their chief rigger. He was to be permanently based at Malcolm's slipway in Port Bannatyne on the Isle of Bute. When he did manage to visit us in Rhu for the first time, he told us the story of the SS *Volundam* and also that he was looking for a house to rent in Port Bannatyne, so he could bring us over to be a family once more. Bear with me dear reader, and once more let this nine-year-old boy turn you over to my dad for his account of the *Volundam* story.

The SS *Volundam* was a Dutch liner of approximately 26,000 tons gross weight. She was carrying mainly evacuee children and their carers attempting to flee from the Nazi invasion of their homeland. She had managed to steam around Scotland and was well down the west coast heading for the Clyde estuary and safety. So near and yet so far, she fell into the periscope view of a U-boat patrolling that area and was promptly torpedoed. She radioed for help, then lowered all her lifeboats full of crew, carers and children. They rowed away from the ship and lay well clear of her while they watched her settle slowly in the water.

When we picked up her distress call we piled on board our tugs, the *Salveda*, the company's main vessel, and the free French *Rene le Besnerais* – we called her the 'Reeny' for short – the Dutch pair *Zee Lewe* and *Zee Hund* and the biggest tug of all, the *Ranger*, and made off at full speed to her rescue. We arrived on the scene and one tug began picking up the survivors, while we pulled alongside of the liner and took hold of the dangling lifeboat falls. It was a long way up to her boat deck from our lowly position. Our best young rope climbers leapt into action and began ascending the lifeboat falls. We older men watched them struggling up the side of the liner.

Horrified we looked up to see a little boy standing on the very edge of the boat deck and looking down at us. He was only about four years old. The climbers and ourselves began shouting to him to stand back from the edge but he paid no attention. The round eyes of the little lad appeared fascinated by the climbers, as if transfixed by the strange struggle they were going through in an attempt to reach him before he plummeted to our deck. Jack Gower made it to the boat deck first and running along behind the child he snatched him back from the edge. Only then did the wee boy burst into tears and it was some time before our lads managed to calm him down.

One small Dutch boy had been missed in the general confusion after the ship was torpedoed. He had been left behind to wander alone, around the huge, empty, sinking ship. Being a Dutch boy, he did not understand English and with all these men shouting at him in a strange language it was a bit too much for the poor wee thing.

Due to her proximity to the west of Scotland's coastline, we were able to reach the ship very quickly and install pumps to keep her afloat. The pumps managed so well it was decided to tow her to Kaimes bay on the Island of Bute. To the locals this was known as Port Bannatyne bay and was the best protected beach on the island.

We were not always successful in our attempts to rescue sinking ships. Sometimes we were forced to beach them on the Irish coast or on the Hebrides islands. These were treacherous locations, infamous for bad weather and sometimes we were forced to withdraw and watch helplessly while the ships sank. The *Volundam* was an exception for so severely damaged a ship but we were blessed with calm weather and got her safely up on the sand in the centre of Port Bannatyne bay.

It's a strange thing about torpedoes; some will blow half the side out of a ship and send her to the bottom in minutes, while others will misfire and do little damage. Still others will explode but do so little critical damage that comparatively small vessels manage to stay afloat. The best example of the latter must be the *Blair Spey*, a small vessel of about 2,000 tons gross. This ship must have broken the heart of the U-boat commander who attacked her. She took the first torpedo in her bows, the second amidships and the third at her stern. Perfect shooting, yet she continued to float. We soon had her in tow and with our pumps coping with the ingress of water we beached her in Port Bannatyne bay.

I managed to get rented accommodation for my family to come to Port Bannatyne to be with me. Before they arrived, the *Coronda* had been re-floated and moored at the Tail of the Bank (the mouth of the Clyde) to await her turn to go up the Clyde for repairs. The *Volundam* had also been temporarily made seaworthy and removed from the bay. Bobby will tell you that the *Blair Spey* was still there, so I will let him describe things as he saw them when he first arrived.

I was still nine years old when I saw Port Bannatyne for the very first time. On the north side of the bay and by far the furthest inshore lay a massive ship called the *Ashantian*. Her bows almost reached the road which ran around the bay. Directly amidships was a huge hole in her side that a double-decker bus could have driven through. Dad told me she had been part of a convoy attacked by a U-boat and the gallant little corvette HMS *Gloxinia* joined in the battle to save the merchantmen. The oil tanker SS *Stratford* was torpedoed and sunk. Many of her crew were left struggling in the water and the corvette was reluctant to use depth charges, which would kill them all instantly. The *Ashantian* was next to be hit by one torpedo amidships and the corvette found herself under attack. She was forced to use her depth charges to drive the U-boat off. Young though I was, I remember thinking how amazing it was that the salvage company had managed to get her safely ashore, for she had the biggest hole in her side anyone had ever seen. Behind her lay the tiny *Blair Spey* with three small holes in her side such as Dad has already described. Further along the north shoreline was a ship painted in Royal Naval grey; she was called the *Newcastle*. She too had been torpedoed. Next to her was half a ship, called simply the 'Greek boat'. She was carrying a full load of timber, which Dad said had helped keep half of her afloat, after the bow section sank. Although the *Coronda* had gone, the high water mark around the beach was a conglomerate of her hardened oil and every day for some time we would come across the dead bodies of gulls, cormorants and other seabirds which had perished due to the pollution.

'Diver!' the pathologist said loudly, and I came to with a start. He and One-eyed Fergie were standing by the open door of the waiting room, along with the court officer who had taken us to lunch the day before.

'You were miles away,' the pathologist continued, smiling indulgently. 'Time to go for something to eat once again.' I stood up and followed them out. I was glad of the walk to the hotel to stretch my legs after sitting for so many hours in that small waiting room. As we walked along I found myself marvelling once again at probably my father's biggest escape of all as I pondered over the story of the 'Captain's Bomb'.

6

The Captain's Bomb

Dad came home one night after being away for nearly three weeks on a salvage job. He was in a drunken state, worse than I had ever seen before. He went straight to his bed and slept right through Saturday night and all of Sunday morning. Eventually he awoke, got dressed and told Mum and I the following story, which horrified us both and from that moment onwards made us worry all the more whenever he set off on another salvage mission. Here is his story.

When we got on board the *Reeny*, we were told we were going to the aid of a Royal Naval destroyer that had been bombed in the Irish Sea. We steamed for two days before we came across her, way down close to the southern tip of Ireland. She was one of the old Tribal Class destroyers, a twin-funnelled steam ship, of World War I vintage. We drew alongside and our first thoughts were that she did not appear to be seriously damaged. There was a strange silence about her as she wallowed in the sea. We climbed on board and nary a seaman showed his face as we did so. She appeared to be as deserted as the *Marie Celeste*. Her engine room was dry, the engines lay silent with the telegraph plainly showing 'Stop engines'. There was nobody down there. Her stoke hold was the same. Her fires still burned, but only just, and not enough to make steam. She appeared completely watertight and wallowed side-on to the weather in fine form.

We set about the task of taking her in tow and just then the *Zee Hund* came alongside. Mr Thomas climbed aboard followed by two naval officers. We suggested to our boss that we could easily fire up the destroyer's own engines to bring her in. We told him we had men in the engine room and others in the stoke hold standing by to build up her fires. Thomas said, 'Just carry on setting up tow ropes. Let the "Reeny" and the *Zee Hund* bring her in.' He moved away from us and he and the two naval officers began discussing something in private. Shortly after that, he came back to us. 'We won't be using the ship's own engines, so bring everybody up out of the stoke hold and engine room *now*.' He stressed the word NOW.

This was unlike our boss; usually he would ponder over the merits of any suggestion put to him by any one of us, but not this time. We called the lads to come up on deck, just when they were getting ready to shovel fresh coal on the fires and get steam up to start the engines. It seemed strange to us salvage men that we were going to tow her all the way, when we could have started her own engines and sailed her safely into port. There was no argument about it, however; Mr Thomas was the boss, but it all seemed a bit of a mystery.

We thought we would be towing her into Liverpool or one of the Clyde ports. Instead Mr Thomas told us to make for a deep water buoy that lay about three miles off Port Bannatyne bay. We arrived at the buoy and moored the old destroyer up to it. Once we had her secure, Mr Thomas asked us to go into the ship's main mess room, as the naval officers wanted to talk to us. We were bewildered by this, nothing like it had ever happened to us before. This job was getting stranger by the minute.

It was a motley crew that sat down by the mess room tables.

There were the Liverpool men, Albert Gower, his twenty-one-year-old son Jack, Henry Brae and Jack Duckworth, the two divers, Davy Bell and Peter Taylor, the Irishmen, Eddie Docherty and Danny Mcarra, the Aussie, Digger Foley, and the Western Islanders Donald Mcintyre, Donald Mcleish, and Donald Gillies and the Shetlander, myself.

Mr Thomas came in with the two officers.

'Well lads,' he said, 'You have done a good job, and,' he indicated one of the officers, 'this is the destroyer's captain and he would like to thank you all personally.'

The captain, a very young-looking two-ringed lieutenant stepped forward. 'Well chaps,' he said in a very pompous English voice. 'I want to thank you all for saving my ship. If my ship had been lost, it would have meant the end of my career. The Admiralty are most unforgiving when a captain loses his ship.'

His voice droned on and on, and we were wondering what the hell he was talking about – his ship was perfectly seaworthy and in no danger of being lost as far as we could see. The absence of a crew seemed to be the only drawback, which might have spelt danger for the ship.

'And so' he finally wound up, 'I think it right and proper I should reward you all by allowing you to "splice the mainbrace" aboard my ship. Steward!'

A small man appeared suddenly, carrying a heavy barrel, which he placed on an empty table in front of the captain. He hurried away and was back almost instantly with an armful of half-pint glasses which he began dishing out to all of us. The little man wore a white steward's coat and on his head he had a sailor's hat with just three letters on it: HMS. No ship's name – this of course was normal with all naval crews throughout the duration of the war.

'Bring your glasses to the table,' said the captain, 'and the steward will measure out a tot of rum for each of you. I must caution you, however, Navy rum is very strong and I would advise you to add two parts water to one part rum. That is the way our sailors drink it.'

Eddie Docherty grunted 'Ugh!' and shuddered violently. The captain noticed and went on, 'Of course you chaps can suit yourselves, however you like it.'

Needless to say, we all took it straight. Half an hour later we were beginning to feel quite merry. Some story-telling was taking place and some jokes were being bandied about.

The captain joined in the celebrations, albeit without touching a drop of alcohol. He called to the steward once again saying, 'Freshen up the chaps' glasses and bring some boxes of cigars from the wardroom.'

An amazing transformation was taking place right before our very eyes. The pompous, boring young captain had changed into a 'hail fellow well met' mate of ours. An hour later we were tucking into fresh sandwiches, drinking excellent coffee, laced with black rum, and smoking the captain's cigars. Donald Gillies was playing imaginary bagpipes. He strode up and down between the tables, his fingers playing phantom notes. Out of the side of his mouth came a fearful sound that did bear a slight resemblance to the sound of the pipes.

'Heeterum hoterum, heeterum hoterum!' he roared as he went by us. I swear I saw the captain wince but he said not a word.

After a while Donald finally gave up and sat back down to his drink again. Mr Thomas stood up and called out for our attention. He began to explain that the captain wanted us to carry on with our party, but he wondered if we could do him a favour first, then return to the mess hall for more drinks. To a man the lads shouted out, 'Sure thing captain, we are your men, what do you want us to do for you?' The mood of the men suggested that they would probably have killed for him by that time.

'Now chaps' the captain said, 'my crew were all young and inexperienced, this was their first real test after we were commissioned. We were attacked by bombers, I set a defensive zig-zag course while my gunners engaged the Germans. Neither of us gained an advantage for some time. We could not hit them and meanwhile two of their bombs splashed close by the side of the ship harmlessly. A third bomb, however, hit the main deck forward but failed to explode. The problem I am faced with is the fact that we're not sure where this bomb finished up. We think we know where it is but we're not sure.'

Eddie Docherty leapt to his feet exclaiming loudly, 'We'll find it for you captain, won't we lads?' This was greeted with instant approval by all of us.

'Thank you,' the captain said. 'My first officer here will show you where we think it is.' He indicated the young sub-lieutenant standing beside him. 'We have a bomb disposal squad, probably on their way to us at this very moment, but it would be a great help if we could find it, and get it up on deck, so they can carry it off as soon as they arrive. Thereafter, we could all have a real whing-ding of a party, for the rest of the evening.'

We all filed out of the mess following the young officer and I can tell you there were one or two of us who were not too steady on our feet. A blind man could have found that bomb. A furrow along the main deck had been gouged out of the steel-work. Then a clean hole showed where it had ploughed through a vertical bulkhead, into the petty officers' mess room. We had to take turns to look inside.

There was a lot of blood on the floor and splintered wood-work everywhere. The young officer whispered, 'Two of our petty officers died in here although the bomb didn't explode.'

The opposite bulkhead had a corresponding hole clean through it and the bomb had descended into the stoke hold and was obviously buried in the bunkers of coal – the ship's fuel.

'We think it may be among the coal,' the officer said sheepishly. We climbed down, and arming ourselves with shovels, began digging through the bunkers and none too gently either. The general idea appeared to be to get the job done quickly and get back to the party. Stokers themselves never worked as furiously as we did.

Then Albert Gower let out a whoop. 'Here's the bitch!' And so it was. The tail fins were exposed, but we were not prepared for the size of it. This was a big, big bomb. A rather hot debate began as to how we would get it up the rather narrow companionway stairs. We had stirred up so much coal dust that it appeared as if we were in a dense fog, and we all stopped arguing and began laughing when we looked at each other's faces. We looked like chimney sweeps. Each one of us had been wiping our mouths and our eyes as we dug down through the coal. The result was a broad band of white around our mouths and round circles of white around our eyes. We now looked like the black and white minstrel show. Al Jolson himself would have been proud of us. The laughing soon stopped and we returned to the debate of the best way to get the bomb out of there. It was decided it had to go up the stairway backwards. We all agreed we would be safe so long as we did not bump the nose cone. For the rest of my life I would give an involuntary shudder when remembering the treatment we gave that bomb. It was bumped up each step, the tail fins were rattled against the rails. When we got the damned thing outside, some of us lost our footing and dropped it with an almighty clatter on the deck and Eddie Docherty fell sprawling, legs and arms akimbo, right across it. Donald Gillies hauled him off angrily saying, 'What the hell are you doing man, you could set it off, diving on top of it like that!'

Eddie scrambled upright. 'I didn't dive on the fucking thing!' he roared, bristling with rage. 'I tripped and fell on it.' We left them arguing and dragged the bomb close by the ship's side and as we did so I noticed Mr Thomas and the two officers standing right on the extreme end of the stern. The thought struck me that this was a small ship and this was a large bomb, and remembering the *Coronda* I knew they would have perished just the same as us if it had gone off. We felt we had now completed our favour for the captain, so we returned to the main mess hall. It was one hell of a party from then on.

The captain was as good as his word and we were all treated like royalty for the rest of the night. As soon as I got ashore I went into the inn on my way home for a pint of beer and after my first swallow I wanted to sing a song. Charlie Walker took one look at me and I swear he dived down into his cellar to water down his beer. I think he soon realised his mistake, for I was almost legless in no time. Old Charlie came over and advised me to get myself upstairs to my bed. From that day to this I still shudder when I think of what we did that day. We never did find out what happened to the crew of that ship, nor what eventually happened to the captain's bomb.

7

SS Politician

In the early years of World War II the SS *Politician* lay wrecked on the seabed, close to the isle of Eriskay, in the Hebrides off the west coast of Scotland. The Liverpool and Glasgow Salvage Company were in attendance on the waters around her. She lay in fairly shallow water and at low tide most of her superstructure was above the sea level. She was not a war casualty, having been driven onto rocks by gale force winds. The salvage divers were below, appraising her overall condition, with the possibility of raising her, or at the least salvaging her cargo and some of the precious metal of the wreck itself to aid the war effort.

One of the divers, Peter Taylor, stood on the top rung of the diving ladder still fully dressed in his hard hat diving suit. Only his front light had been removed so he could speak to his linesman. The linesman turned and called up to the foreman rigger standing on the deck of a lifting craft above them.

'Attie, Peter is feeling unwell.' The foreman rigger, my father, quickly climbed down into the diving boat and bent over to peer in through the front light at Peter.

'What's the problem Pete?' he asked. A powerful smell of alcohol wafted past his nostrils, driven out of the helmet by the diving pumps still feeding the suit.

'I don't feel so good,' Peter slurred. Dad turned to the linesmen.

'Get him undressed and below into his bunk before Mr Thomas sees him; he's steaming drunk.' Dad helped the men steer the staggering diver into the cabin of the diving boat, then he climbed quickly back on board the lifting craft to assure himself that the salvage supervisor, Mr Thomas, had not witnessed the event.

After that day the survey of the wrecked vessel carried on as usual and Peter was his old self-confident diver again. He had not said a word to any of the salvage crew as regards what had happened to him that day. Dad never asked any questions either, as Peter and he were very good friends and often had a drink together when they were ashore. Dad, however, kept a close watch on Peter every time he came on board to report for work, but Peter was a model of sobriety during that time and so it came about one day that Dad watched him descend into the depths apparently as sober as a judge. At the end of the day's diving Peter returned to the surface in such a state that he could barely climb up the diving ladder. He was as drunk as a lord and this time Mr Thomas and Dad watched the efforts being made to get Peter safely on board. Mr Thomas turned to Dad.

'I thought you were keeping an eye on him where drink is concerned.'

Dad knew instantly that his boss must have been aware of the first incident, although he had not said one word about it to anyone.

'I swear to God he went down this morning without a drop in him, as far as I could see.'

'He has several drops in him now,' said Mr Thomas sarcastically. 'He has proved in the past he can hold his liquor. So God knows how much he has swallowed to get in a state like that. Anyway Arthur, when he's sober tomorrow, tell him I want to see him.'

'Right, will do,' said Dad. 'But first I'll find out where the hell he got the drink from, for believe me, he was stone cold sober when he went down this morning.'

The next morning three men sat in the chief engineer's cabin aboard the *Ranger*: my father and the company's chief diver David Bell, plus Peter Taylor.

'You are in a lot of trouble Pete,' said Dad. 'The boss wants to see you this morning.'

'I know it,' Peter answered. 'Stupid, yes, but I couldn't resist it.'

Dave Bell clapped the crestfallen man on the shoulder.

'Tell us what happened,' he said. 'Maybe we can help.'

So Peter told them his story.

'On my first dive, I reported she had broken her hull across a ridge of rock. I could see inside her double bottoms, under her aft hold. On the second day I realised she had settled during the night and with her list to starboard she had split her plating above the double bottoms. Her side plating had now been pressed inwards, leaving a big enough hole to let me through into her hold. I didn't let anybody know I had gone inside. While I was inside I came across her cargo of crates of the finest Scotch whisky. I stood there for some time considering whether I could open a crate and maybe hide away a bottle or two. I decided it was not worth taking a chance with my job.

'While standing there I was suddenly aware of a booming noise above me. It dawned on me that my exhaust air must be getting trapped against the deck head somewhere just forward of where I was standing. Damn me, when I moved forward, I found her starboard list had caused the stacked up crates to slide sideways. Not enough to cause them to collapse to the floor of the hold but just enough to form an upward staircase. When I climbed up the crates, my helmet broke surface. My exhaust air had formed a substantial air pocket against the underside of the tween decks. The following day, I tucked a small tommy bar into my belt before going down. I climbed back up the crates and when my helmet came above the water. I prised open one crate, took out a bottle and opened it. I laid it on the topmost crate, which was above the water level. I then used the tommy bar to unscrew my front light, so I could have a damn good swallow of that gorgeous liquid. I put the top back on the bottle but left it sitting there in the dry, screwed back my front light and clambered down, intending to carry on with my work. In fact I did carry on with my work, but after a while, I thought, no harm in popping back for another wee swig, so I did. By the time I was due to surface, I was well into the second bottle. I didn't go near it for days after that first time.

'You see, I thought Attie had covered up for me and Thomas had no idea what had happened. I know now that Attie thought so too. Well I can tell you, those days I didn't go near it were pure murder. I could visualise that half-full bottle sitting in the dry on the topmost crate. In the end it was too much for me, it was like the proverbial nectar of the gods and here I was surrounded by a full cargo of the stuff. Okay, the second time, I went right over the score but what the hell, we spend most of our time working so close to death, or actually bringing up dead men, so they can be given a decent burial. It would drive any man to drink.'

Both Dad and Dave were partly amused by Peter's story. They were also very moved by the last of it. They resolved to go together to see Mr Thomas on Peter's behalf and this they did. Dad reckoned their boss would let Peter off with a reprimand. In this he was correct. Peter was treated to a right royal lecture, which held more substance with regard to his own safety, removing his front light under water and getting sozzled with drink, while working in an environment that normally does not support human life. The supervisor finished up by warning him against any similar future conduct, which would have dire consequences regarding his employment with the salvage company.

Mr Thomas was a man who understood his hard-working, hard-drinking salvage men and whenever he could he turned a Nelson eye on their escapades. From then on the work went smoothly ahead on the *Politician*. She was temporarily sealed off aft, where Peter had entered her, by using a thick rubber patch. This was held in place by bolts fired through her side plating using a Cox's bolt-driving gun. Her holds were also sealed at deck level and she was pumped full of compressed air and successfully floated off the rocks. It was decided she was too sorely damaged to attempt to tow her for any distance, so the tugs pulled her into the sound of Eriskay.

She was beached on a sand bar with the intention of rigging strengthening bars across the temporary rubber patch, but even that short journey had caused too much extra failure in the metal under her aft hold. She was finally cut in half and the forward undamaged part of her was towed away. The after-part was left behind, with its cargo of special whisky. This was the ship that inspired Sir Compton McKenzie to write his famous book, *Whisky Galore*.

8

Port Bannatyne

Our little family stayed for a short while in two houses in Port Bannatyne. Finally we moved into number 45 Marine Road. This self-contained flat was immediately above our landlord Charlie Walker's inn. All our front windows looked down onto the beach, virtually in the dead centre of the port. If we had wished, we could have thrown a ball across Marine Road onto the beach from our front windows. I was still nine years old and my kid sister was five but for some reason Mum still kept us off school. One day I set off into the open country inland. I carried a mouse trap with me and the idea was I would catch a rabbit in the mouse trap to help Mum with the meat rationing. Ah! The innocence of youth. I remember walking home in the early evening, the sun still shining brightly, and as I walked I began composing a little song to commemorate my own foolishness. It was set to a popular tune of that era. 'You can't catch a rabbit with a mouse trap, mouse trap. You may be able to catch, a teeny weeny mouse but you can't catch a rabbit with a mouse trap.'

Shortly after that Mum decided to send Isobel and I back to school and the happy freedom days were over. We were to join local youngsters and evacuee children from Port Glasgow, Paisley, Greenock and Glasgow itself. The school was in an old church, called the Strain Hall. A certain Miss Young took the five-year-olds, while we older kids would be taught by Mr J.R. Stewart. Both teachers had been sent from Glasgow because of the number of evacuees on the island. I was a very sad little lad when I first went to school there, because of all the time I had lost in Shetland, Edinburgh, Rhu and Bute itself. I was placed in a class of eight-year-olds. As a result I was looked upon by my own age group as a bit of a backward lad to start with. However, I soon caught up with my own age group and proved I was normal after all.

One night Dad came home and said to me, 'Tomorrow I want you to watch out for an old farmer who comes into the town on a horse and cart. He sells buttermilk, so give him this jug.'

He handed me a large enamel jug. 'I want you to say, fill it up please, it's for Attie, and say nothing else.' My mother lifted the jug out of my arms and said, 'What are you going to do with such an amount of buttermilk Attie?'

Dad smiled and winked at mum. 'You will see,' he said. He turned to me. 'Now, remember just say, fill it up please, it's for Attie, and pay him. Hold this in your other hand but don't give it to him.' He handed me a small brown canvas bag, saying, 'He might take the bag from you, or he might not, let him decide.'

The next day, a Saturday, I watched out of our front window at the time the old farmer was due. Sure enough he came in sight, the horse trotting along briskly, and pulled up beside a group of people obviously waiting for his arrival. I hurried down the stairs and ran along the pavement to join the queue. By the time I arrived, the old farmer was standing at the back of his cart, which had two large metal cans sitting on a ledge at the very back end. They were held securely in place by a chain stretched across their middle. Each can had a shiny brass tap at its bottom. Johnnie Dick, the old farmer, was tall, broad-shouldered and with a bulging stomach, which was at odds with his old, but very muscular, frame. He wore the biggest pair of tackety boots I have ever seen.

I stood at the back of the queue and watched the antics of the big man. He was deliberately using the considerable bulk of his own body to hide something he was giving to certain customers. He would take a very slight glance at the next customer, who was obviously whispering something to him. Without a sound, he would shake his head vigorously, grab their container and fill it. The next person might also try a whisper. Still without a word, he would snatch their jug and turn his whole body side on, to give that customer something nobody else was supposed to see.

When my turn came, I held the brown canvas bag down at my left side. I lifted the large enamel jug very slightly with my right hand and found myself whispering, 'Fill it up please, it's for Attie.' From a great height above me, the big head hardly turned but the eyes swivelled downwards. He took the jug gently from me, filled it with buttermilk and replaced it in my arms. I paid him and struggled home with the big jug. I have no idea what took place between my dad and the farmer after that but I can guess. Filled with buttermilk that jug was too heavy for a wee boy. I was given a much smaller one the following week. This time the small jug was whipped out of my hand and the brown canvas bag followed suit. The farmer swung side on to hide what he was giving me.

Back in our house I showed Mum a round pat of about a quarter of a pound of fresh butter floating on top of the buttermilk and two large duck eggs inside the brown canvas bag.

At that time, we boys used to play football in the road in front of our house. We played with a tennis ball and nobody seemed to mind. It's true the ball often went over onto the beach but we would run down the steps at the side of Mr Alexander's boat shed to retrieve it. On a Saturday night we would play quite

51

late and being summertime we had plenty of light. We would stop playing to allow the local bus to go by and we always kept a lookout for Johnnie Dick, the old farmer, returning from Rothesay.

On a Saturday he would sell his butter, eggs, buttermilk and occasional chickens all the way to Rothesay. He then used to head for his favourite pub and get blind drunk. His faithful old horse would stand patiently waiting outside for hour after hour, until some of the locals would carry him out. They never tried to put him up on the seat, he was always too drunk for that, so they usually laid him on his back across the width of the cart. The moment the locals headed back into the bar, the old horse would take off. He knew where he was going and he was desperate to get back to his own stable.

He had three miles to travel from Rothesay to Port Bannatyne and another three miles to Ettrick bay, on the west side of the island, and then one more mile to the farm and his stable. We would be playing up and down the main road when the old horse would come in sight at a full gallop. We soon got out of his way; he would go raging past, the huge hobnailed boots, showing only their soles, the only indication that old Johnnie Dick was aboard. This became a regular occurrence on a Saturday night.

The port's post office was next to the inn and was run by two old ladies. They were spinster sisters and were very generous and genteel. Upon receiving a telegram, which had to be delivered, one of them would come out and offer a sixpence to any boy who was willing to cycle to the address. I earned many a sixpence by living so close to the post office.

One day I was running through the close beside our house when I saw a brown paper bag ahead of me. As I reached it I pretended it was a football and I was about to score a goal for

Scotland against England. I lashed out with my right foot and the bag flew up in the air. Instantly, I was the Scottish goalkeeper about to make the save that would win us the match. I clutched hold of the bag and continued my run to our back door.

Within seconds I realised the bag was not empty. I opened it to find a fortune in one pound notes inside. To be more precise, I counted twenty-two pounds in all. At that time this was the equivalent of more than five men's wages for a week. My dad was home when I got to the house, so I showed him what I had found. He took me to the local police station to report it. The policeman asked my dad if I wanted a reward and dad said it would only be fair that I should be rewarded for my honesty. The money turned out to belong to the two old dears who ran the post office and they were so grateful to have it returned to them, that from then onwards I was singled out to deliver telegrams more often than any other boy who might be present at the time. My mother also bought me a new suit of short trousers and jacket with the reward.

Old Mr Alexander lived in the next house to ours. He and his wife had no family of their own, but they did have a little terrier dog called Mac, which was treated like a son by the old couple. One day Mrs Alexander met Mum and said to her, 'You know, it was Mac's birthday last week and he was so pleased, because he got a birthday card from my sister's wee collie dog in Glasgow.'

The old man himself suffered from failing eyesight and at night he used to come out to the back green looking for his wee dog. He would stand for ages peering out at the gathering darkness and every now and then he would shout out loudly, 'Mac!' The little dog would be sitting no more than six feet in front of him and staring up at his master's face with an evil looking grin

53

that showed all of his teeth. He would remain there like that for the longest time, while the old man continued to shout 'Mac!' every so often. The wicked wee dog would rise up eventually and trot forward and announce his arrival by rubbing against the old man's leg. 'Oh! There you are, my wee lamb,' the old man would say, as he gathered the dog in his arms. 'I wish you would not go so far away at night, for it makes Daddy so worried that something might have happened to you.' And up the stairs he would go, carrying the wicked wee dog. The next night there would be a repeat performance.

Mr Alexander had his own small boat-hiring business, which was a summertime-only occupation aimed at the considerable tourist trade the Isle of Bute enjoyed. He had a set of moorings that lay off the shore immediately in front of his house. Anchored to these moorings were twelve of the finest clinker-built rowing boats I have ever seen. They were lovingly looked after all through the winter months in a covered enclosure inside Malcolm's yacht-repairing yard. There, the old man would varnish them and fit them all with snowy-white piping around the outside of their gunnels to protect them from the rough and ready holidaymakers who would hire them in the summer. They all had romantic names painted in gold leaf across their transoms, such as *Myrtle*, *Mayflower*, *Maria*, etc.

The old man asked me if I would like to work for him in the mornings and afternoons, before and after school, during the summer. I accepted gladly, because it would give me the chance to fish from the moored boats on my own, instead of being part of a crowd of boys trying to find space on Malcolm's slipway or the stone quay. At the same time, I would be earning money. In the mornings the old man would open up his little shed, built on a platform halfway down the sea wall, and he and I would take out a small, one-man dinghy, which we both could carry easily down the wooden steps and out onto the low wooden pier, which the old man had built himself, barely above the sea level. Once placed in the water, I would climb aboard, armed with brushes, dry cloths and a bucket. I would row out to the moored boats and chase the seagulls off them. I then had to clean each one, by throwing over the side all the balls of chaff the gulls had regurgitated, after their meals of grain, eaten the day before. Next I had to wash and clean their droppings – God they were messy birds. I would then tow four clean boats ashore and make them fast to the little pier, according to whether the tide was ebbing or flowing. I could then return to the remaining boats and fish from them, until such time as the holidaymakers made off with the first four on hire. The next four would then be brought in and again I could return to my fishing. When all twelve boats were out on hire I could fish to my heart's content from the little one-man dinghy.

There were times when I had another duty to perform. Some of the holidaymakers would pay for a certain time out on a boat and stay out away past the time they had paid for. Instead of coming in and paying the extra, they would row across the bay and abandon the boat on the north shore. I would then set off in the little dinghy and search for it. They were dishonest people but they were not vandals. I always found the boats were unharmed and I would tow them back across the bay to their moorings.

Sometimes I would row alongside one of the wrecked ships, such as the *Ashantian*, before looking for a missing boat, and if the sea was calm and the water clear, I would row through the torpedo hole, to see inside the ship itself. It was always very eerie in there and I was mindful to look under the surface for any underwater hazards.

Down through the clear water, I would see brown fronds of seaweed, waving in the gentle tidal current. Small rock codling and little pollack swam lazily among the fronds. Above and below the surface was a tangled and twisted mass of torn metal, rent in all directions. The water level in there would rise and fall in slow motion with a soft gurgling noise, through the myriad holes and channels of the ruptured metal, and at times it seemed to sigh audibly. In my imagination, it was like the sad sighing of the souls of the men who had lost their lives in that dank, gloomy, cavern of steel.

I did not stay in there for long and once outside I breathed in the clean salty air with a sense of relief. I would then carry on searching for any missing boats along the shoreline.

Old Mr Alexander was a good boss and one of the most contented men I ever met. I never saw him get angry at any time and to watch him smoking his hooked pipe, while he deftly shelled mussels, to sell as bait, along with the fishing lines he hired out, was to watch a man at peace with his world. I knew the only real sadness in the old man's life was the fact that he and his wife had never been able to have any children of their own.

One day, during the school holidays, I was playing on the beach with some of my pals close to the White Pier when one of the lads, Andy Morgan, called us over to see what he had found.

'What do you think it's for?' he asked.

We were looking at a metal tray, which had been sunk in the pebbly beach and stretched all the way from the road until it vanished below the surface of the sea. The tray held about ten rubber cables, grouped together and bound with wire. The cables were about one half inch in diameter and they ran the full length of the tray.

'It must have something to do with the pier,' said Michael Morgan, Andy's younger brother.

I looked at the position of the cables. They did not line up with the pier. I said, 'I don't think so, they go out well to one side of the pier.'

We were standing there, still pondering the purpose of the cables, when Bert Gower came by. He was a big lad, three years older than we were, and to be honest, he was not very bright, in fact for a fifteen-year-old he appeared to have the mentality of a seven-year-old. 'What have you got there?' he asked and on seeing the cables, he exclaimed loudly. 'Great! just the thing for a strong catapult.'

We tried to talk him out of it, but no, he seemed to think we wanted to keep the cables for ourselves. 'I'm taking my share and you can't stop me!' he said belligerently. There was no way we could have stopped him, as he opened up a large penknife and cutting between the binding wires, which were about six feet apart, he removed a length of about four feet.

'I'll have the strongest catapult of all with this,' he said triumphantly, and off he went. We also left the scene as fast as we could go, for fear of the consequences.

Later that evening Bert was arrested and charged with destroying Royal Naval property. He stood trial in Rothesay, was convicted and sentenced to six strokes of the birch on his bare back. Everyone agreed that for a young boy of his mental ability this was a travesty of justice. Nevertheless, the sentence was carried out.

A few days later, on our way home from school, we saw what appeared to be a man dressed in a tight-fitting rubber suit apparently standing on the surface of the water close by the White Pier. This was our first sighting of the 'X' craft – the little submarines that later would attack and cripple the mighty German battleship the *Tirpitz*. We then learned that the cables young Bert had cut up were there to supply the power to charge up the tiny submarine's batteries. On a hillside above the White Pier

stood the Hydro Hotel which the Royal Navy had comman-
deered and renamed HMS *Varbell*. The sailors billeted there were
mainly the working parties and crews of the midget submarines
and the full-size submarines, which lay alongside their mother
ship HMS *Cyclops*, anchored in Rothesay bay. Lord Haw-Haw
broadcast one night from Germany saying, 'Do not think for a
moment that we are ignorant of the fact that HMS *Cyclops* lies
in Rothesay bay surrounded by her submarines. Expect a visit
quite soon from the Luftwaffe.' This threat never materialised
during the remaining years of the war but the fear was forever
present.

9

Heigh-ho Silver!

In the winter of 1942, at eleven years of age, I first went to work for Miss Mary McKinnon, of Bannatyne Mains Farm. This young woman, in her early twenties, practically ran the farm on her own. Only occasionally did she have help from her older brother Donald, who also ran another farm at Ardmaleish. Myself and Andy and Michael Morgan were given the job of milk boys, delivering milk to Mary's customers in the port and the nearby village of Ardbeg. I loved to get up to the farm in the early morning, before anyone else was around, and get the old grey mare Silver out of her stable and harness her into the milk cart. This was a two-wheeled cart, similar to Johnnie Dick's, except this one carried two churns of the sweetest fresh milk.

One morning I was just finishing adjusting the traces when the horse gave me the fright of my life by dropping to her knees with a crash. The wooden trams smashed into the ground but luckily they did not break. The mare scrambled wildly back to her feet and whinnied in fear. Mary had seen what had happened as she came out of the farmhouse. I thought the horse had been suddenly taken ill but Mary knew differently.

'That damn horse will break the trams some day,' she said, examining them carefully. I also felt around the ends of the trams but other than chipped paint they were fine.

'What was the matter with her?' I asked.

'Nothing's the matter with her,' Mary answered. 'The stupid bitch just falls asleep and drops. I'll tell you what you will need to do Bobby. First thing in the mornings you will need to put a rope halter on her and ride her up and down the road to waken her up before you put her in the cart.'

From that day onwards, I would arrive even earlier and ride the mare along Bannatyne Mains road and back to the farm before putting her in the cart. When all was ready, with the full milk churns in their place, we three boys would climb up on the cart and wait for Mary. She always arrived wearing riding breeches and boots, in fact for the years I knew her, I never once saw her wear a skirt. Silver would trot briskly down into Port Bannatyne and pull up of her own accord at our first stop. Mary would stand at the back of the cart and measure out the milk. Some old folk only required a half pint per day. Other families wanted a half gallon. Andy, Michael and I would run back and forth delivering the milk and old Silver knew when to move on to the next stop.

Sometimes I would arrive at the farm in the early morning to be greeted by a lowing call of distress from the byre. Going in to check what was happening I would often find a new-born calf lying in the muck trough, and the mother unable to reach it, because she was chained in her stall. I would alert Mary and we would soon have the mother and calf in a straw enclosure in the barn. If the calf was female, she would usually be allowed to grow up. If male, it was sent to the slaughter house within days of its birth. We kept one stud bull of around four years of age and a young male calf of just over a year old, called Wee Geordie, who would one day take over as stud bull. This was the usual set up on all the farms.

Six months later, I was riding Silver up the farm road one

morning and I came upon the field where Wee Geordie always lived by himself. The young bull was nowhere to be seen. At the bottom of the hill, I came across the smashed remains of the five-barred gate which gave access to his field. I pulled up the mare, turned her around and made off at a gallop. There was no way I was going to take the chance of hanging around there with an angry bull on the loose. Arriving back at the farm, I met Mary, Andy and Michael coming out of the stables. For once the normally unflustered Mary showed signs of real concern when I gave her the bad news.

'We must find him,' she said. 'God knows what he might get up to, he could easily maim, or even kill some poor beggar he might come across.' She turned to Andy. 'Go back in the stables Andy and get three hook poles.' Andy came back carrying the hook poles. 'Now listen boys,' Mary said, 'I don't want you taking any chances, remember, it is one thing to control a bull when you already have the pole hooked in his nose ring. It is an entirely different thing when he is loose and able to run about. What you must do, is be prepared to get behind a tree or any obstacle if he comes after you. Don't try to hook his nose ring under any circumstances.'

All three of us assured Mary we would do what she told us.

So we set off on foot down Bannatyne Mains road and past the wrecked gate. We scanned the road ahead carefully, especially the junction with the Ettrick Bay road, but both roads were clear. Now we had to decide which way the rogue bull had gone. Had he gone back towards the port, or on towards Ettrick Bay? It was just then I spotted something a fair bit up the road and close by the north wall. It turned out to be a pile of the bull's droppings, so we headed that way. Michael was walking along closest to the wall and suddenly, pointing over it, he said, loudly, 'There he is!' and right enough in the field, among farmer Malcolm's dairy cows was Wee Geordie. He was in the process of doing what bulls do, to as many cows as possible. He must have jumped over the wall to get to them.

'Oh my God!' Mary exclaimed. 'The little bastard will have them all in calf.'

Now this was serious stuff, for Malcolm also sold milk to his own customers in the port and unlike goats, which can still be milked while carrying kids, dairy cows stop producing milk as soon as they are in calf.

An agreement was eventually reached between farmer Malcolm and Mary whereby they would share the milk yield of the two farms and put their respective customers on rationing, until Malcolm's herd came back on stream. They would also share the calves, when they were born. Wee Geordie came home with us, as gentle as a little lamb. He had lost the violent rage that had caused him to smash his way out of his field. He was so successful in this, his first attempt as a stud bull, that shortly after the calves were born, the old bull was sent to the slaughterhouse and Wee Geordie took over his job.

One beautiful spring morning, with all the birds singing their hearts out and greeting the rising sun as it appeared above the eastern horizon, I threw a sack across Silver's back and leapt aboard. I had arrived early as usual but two calves had been born overnight and I had initially helped Mary to clean them up, until Andy and Mike arrived and took over. Mary said, 'Bobby, you take Silver for a short run only. We're away behind time this morning and if we can't make it up you boys will be late for school.'

I gripped the rope halter and urged the mare forward with a tap of my heels on her sides. The mare was in good form and off we went at a brisk trot down the road. Mary had warned me not to push her too hard when riding her in the mornings. She explained that Silver was now more than middle aged, so I must not let her break into a gallop at any time. This morning I had to hold her in check, or she would have galloped for the sheer joy of it. It only took a mile down the road for her to slow down to walking pace once more. From my elevated position on the mare's back, I could see right round the bend towards Ardmaleish. Coming towards me on foot was Donald McKinnon and he was leading the stallion, Black Beauty. He had not yet seen me and was plodding along with his head down.

I knew that Silver was in season and the stallion must have picked up her scent. He suddenly reared up and tore the halter out of Donald's hand. He broke into a gallop towards me and I felt real fear, for he was an enormous horse. Donald saw me and began shouting.

'Get off her and shove her in a field!' He was now screaming the words, 'GET OFF HER AND SHOVE HER IN A FIELD!'

As luck would have it, I was close by the gate to the east field. I leapt off the mare and opened the gate, whacked her rump and she trotted into the field. I left the gate open and prepared to take evasive action. The stallion's hooves thundered on the road surface as he neared me but he saw the mare enter the field and instead of continuing on to the gate, he jumped sideways over the hawthorn hedge. His chest crashed through the small upper branches of the hedge, spraying blood as he did so. The mare saw him coming at her and she lowered her head right down to the ground and arched her back to receive him. He reared up on his hind legs and his front hooves came down on the mare's back with a sickening crash. The deed was done.

Donald and I closed the gate and left them to it.

'I thought you would all be away with the milk,' said Donald gruffly as we walked back towards the farm.

'We should have been,' I answered, 'except we had two new

calves to look after and Andy and Mike chose this morning to sleep in.'

Donald said nothing for a few minutes and strode along with his head down as usual. 'Do you know what this means now?' he asked.

'No,' I answered.

'It means we will have to hire a horse to pull the milk cart if Silver foals.'

We arrived back at the farm, and to say Mary was annoyed at the news was to put it mildly. She turned on Donald. 'You knew the mare was in season,' she stormed at him. 'You might have made sure we were away before bringing Beauty round.'

Donald was never a man to get excited about anything. 'I expected you to be long gone,' he said, 'but what is done, is done, she might not take, after all she is cracking on a bit and no youngster nowadays.'

Mary shook her head in a sad fashion. 'It is her age that bothers me,' she answered quietly. 'She might take, and trying to foal could just as easily kill her.'

'You worry too much Mary,' Donald said as he walked away. 'Mares are made of strong stuff you know.' He looked over his shoulder at his sister. 'Next year you might have another wee Silver to look after.'

His sister called back at him, 'I might and I might not Donald, for your sake, I hope it turns out all right.'

Donald rounded the gable of the barn and went out of sight but he called back loudly, 'Heigh ho Silver, away!'

The old mare, Silver, continued pulling the milk cart for some time, until it was obvious she was with foal. Thereafter she was rested up and Brandy, another mare hired by Mary, took over. In due course old Silver was delivered of a beautiful coal-black colt. You only had to look at him, with his shining black coat, and see the pride his old mother showed when she nuzzled him, to make you realise that some things are meant to be.

Mary was very tolerant of us, her young male helpers. She also taught us a lot about farm life. One Sunday morning Andy and I were hard at work mucking out the byre, which meant shovelling the fresh muck into barrows, transporting it across the hardened muck of previous years and tipping the barrows over the edge and down into the east field. Here it would solidify and build up until it was three feet higher than the field level. Andy was the real rebel among all of my friends, and would only work for a certain time before he got bored. He would head for the barn and, opening the lids of the metal bins which contained the swede turnip seeds, he filled his pockets.

He had with him his 'gutty', an old Scots word for a catapult, and loading its leather with the hard seeds, he crept up on me, still hard at work barrowing the muck. He fired at me and I felt the sting of the hard little seeds on my face. Naturally I sped off to the barn and armed myself with the same ammunition, for I too had my gutty in my pocket. We both finished up on top of the hardened muck, firing at each other and laughing loudly. We must have made so much noise, it brought Mary out of the farmhouse. The first we knew she was there was when she yelled, 'You pair of young buggers, I have a good mind to give you both a good leathering.'

The following morning, Monday, as we delivered the milk as usual, not a word was said about the day before. Some months later, Mary said, 'Go and see what you young buggers have done to the muck heap in the east field.'

Quite honestly, since then, I have never seen such enormous swede turnips as were growing all over that muck heap.

I don't know where Mary got her patience from but she was more than just tolerant with us wild young boys. She also taught

65

us how to feed the very young calves by showing us how to fill a small pail with warm cow's milk and adding the small calf cake pellets, then adding the thick black treacle called molasses. Once thoroughly mixed, we would place four fingers of one hand in the calf's mouth and it would immediately suck them strongly. Now we had to lower our fingers into the pail, being careful to only let the lips of the calf reach the milk and always make sure that its nostrils stayed above the level of the liquid. This produced the strangest sensation, for the young beast would suck so strongly that by the time the pail was emptied our fingers would be quite numb and pure white in colour.

10

Buncer

Nobody in our family called my Uncle Peter Thomson anything other than 'Buncer'. He was my mother's brother and, like my dad, he was a merchant seaman. Before the war there was a general depression in the Merchant Navy and many seamen found themselves unable to get a berth aboard a ship. They would nevertheless congregate down at the Port of Leith. This both gave them a chance of a job, if a seaman did not turn up when a ship was sailing, or the chance to meet a 'homeward bounder'. This would be a friend of theirs, returning after a long trip and flush with money, money they had been unable to spend on board. The homeward bounder would then invite their less fortunate friends out for a night's drinking. Failing this, and the day wearing on, the desperately poor sailors would club together and pool what little money they did have in what they called a 'tarpaulin muster'. This at least gave them an entrance fee to one of the many pubs the sailors frequented outside the docks and yet another chance one of them might just find a homeward bounder.

One day, Buncer had a great idea, or so he thought at the time. He suggested to the near destitute, stranded sailors, that they should join his Buncer's club. He explained he would allow them plenty of time to pay the initial joining fee of two shillings and sixpence. He of course would be the sole treasurer and he would bank the money, so it gained interest in the meantime. The resultant laughter from the worldly-wise sailors in no way worried my uncle but, needless to say, no one joined his club. From that day onwards he was known as simply 'Buncer'. In 1940 he sailed in an outward-bound convoy from Liverpool. He was the bosun of the *Fort Lennox*, a merchant ship used by the Navy as a fleet auxiliary. They also had a Royal Naval escort of destroyers and corvettes. They were steaming north in the Irish Sea when they came upon a merchant ship being attacked by German aircraft. The Royal Navy opened fire on the German planes and although they were a great distance away, they caused the aircraft to break off the attack.

As the distance decreased between the convoy and the crippled ship, Buncer saw the four-master more clearly. She was burning fiercely at her stern.

'That's the old *Coronda*!' Buncer said. 'My brother-in-law is the bosun aboard her. I hope to God he is all right.'

The convoy sailed on, leaving the lone merchantman to her fate. A few days later, as the convoy neared Iceland, they were very badly mauled by the Luftwaffe. Buncer survived with his ship. He also survived one of the worst tragedies of the war: an attempt to get a convoy through to help the Russians. They were exposed to the full fury of the Luftwaffe, and no help could be expected from the Royal Air Force. At the same time the seas they were sailing through were within easy reach of the deadly 'wolf-packs' of German U-boats. This terrible experience was to prove too much for Buncer and he asked my dad for help. My father spoke to Mr Thomas, who was looking for a first mate for the 'Reeny' at the time and Buncer was given the job. Aunt Margaret and Buncer came to live in Port Bannatyne beside us.

One afternoon, shortly after Buncer took over as mate of the 'Reeny', I was fishing off the end of the stone quay with some of my school friends when my pal George McEwan exclaimed, 'Bobby, look at that!'

I looked up from my bait, which was clearly visible on the bottom through the gin-clear water of the port. Coming around Ardmaleish Point were the two tugs the 'Reeny' and the *Zee Hund*, towing a ship which was half hidden beneath volumes of black smoke. The two tugs were straining hard towards the safety of the clear unbroken sandy beach inside the Point. As we watched, the tugs fanned out away from each other, allowing the burning ship to pass between them and as she took the bottom and rode up the beach a bit, there came a muffled explosion. We saw sheets of flame showing momentarily through the dense smoke. The flames vanished as quickly as they had come, apparently suffocated by the now prodigiously huge swirling cloud arising high above the ship. To us young boys it looked as if a giant genie had been let loose from a huge bottle. We could still see the two tug boats sailing around her and using their power hoses on the burning ship.

The tugs would pass out of our sight behind the ship and reappear as they sailed back into view. Because of their shallow draft they could sail right around the large vessel with no danger of going aground, although the burning merchantman was now solidly resting on the sand.

An hour later we were still watching the ongoing saga when John McEwan, George's older brother, said, 'Look! There's a motor launch leaving her, full of men.' We watched the oncoming motor boat heading our way.

'It's not going for the White Pier,' said Davy Steel, 'it's coming straight here.'

His voice suggested unspeakable horror. All casualties, both wounded and the dead, were usually landed at the White Pier, which lay outside of the port itself.

He was right, the boat was heading straight for us. As it came nearer, we could see all the men were sitting around its gunnel. They appeared to be particularly agitated. They were gesticulating wildly and scooping up a white powder and throwing it on top of a lone man lying struggling in the centre of the boat.

'I know what's happened,' Big John said knowingly. 'He has been badly burned in that last explosion and they're trying to ease his pain.'

We younger boys took on the full horror of this explanation. We did not want to watch as the boat came nearer but we just had to. The victim kept trying to get to his feet but the rest of the men pushed him down again and continued pelting him with the white powder. They were drawing bagfuls out of a large sack in the bottom of the boat. It was then that I recognised Buncer. He was sitting in the stern of the boat and laughing. How could he be *laughing* at such a tragedy? Then I realised they were all laughing. The launch pulled up at the stone steps of the quay and, still laughing, they all clambered up the steps. The young man got to his feet and rather sheepishly smiled as he too left the boat. Only then did we learn that the young man was about to be married and the salvage men were bringing him ashore to celebrate his stag night.

Buncer saw me among the lads on the quay and he said, 'Right now boys, we're going into the blue house for a few drinks and I want wee Bobby to look after our boat till we come back. His pal George will help him and to see fair play, Big John will also be on board, but there could be a few coppers for all of you when we come back because this is a special occasion.'

Having said that, they all headed for Mr McFadyen's inn, about a hundred yards away. We climbed aboard the launch with our fishing lines and carried on fishing. We made no attempt to clean up the boat, which was covered in flour. This was the so called burn-healing powder they had fired over the young man. The burning ship had been carrying a cargo of flour and peanuts in their shells. Dad brought home a huge amount of the monkey nuts, which filled the two bottom drawers of our chest of drawers and stunk out the whole house with the pungent smell of smoke.

Sometimes Buncer would be away for a while and usually Dad went with him. They might be somewhere around the Hebrides rescuing torpedoed ships. I was always excited when they returned, because they always brought something good to eat with them. Depending on the time of year, this might be a box of seagulls' eggs, from the small black-headed gulls to the herring gulls and even the lesser and great black-backed gulls. They also brought survival foodstuff from wrecked lifeboats such as chunks of black chocolate, milk chocolate, small Horlicks tablets and Ovaltine sweets. It was always a change from the monkey nuts we were continually eating out of the chest of drawers.

Where food rationing was concerned, we were much better off than the people back home in Edinburgh. I would go bird-nesting in season and bring home lapwing, curlew, wild duck and pheasant eggs. I always took only one egg from each nest and was lucky to make friends with Gilbert (Gibby) McKirdy, a local lad who knew all the ropes of the sport. We also gathered raspberries, wild strawberries and brambles in the autumn and hazel nuts were plentiful.

At this time Buncer's marriage was on the rocks and he was drinking heavily all the time. Instead of going home to his wife he would head straight for the Blue House of McFadyen's or Charlie Walker's inn. He would then drink there until closing time. Aunt Margaret finally left him and this made him worse than ever.

On our way back from school one afternoon my pal George McEwan and I decided to try a spot of fishing from the end of the White Pier. George's older brother Big John had caught a two-pound codling there the day before. The White Pier was a T-shaped timber-built pier and we were sitting comfortably on the end of its left-hand side. We had caught a few small rock codling and saithe but nothing of any size. We watched the tug 'Reeny' approaching at speed and as usual she began to turn full circle. Normally she would complete the turn and then go hard astern, and with reversed helm stop dead in the centre of the T, barely touching the pier with her fenders. Not this time – she reversed the helm right enough, then instead of going full astern, she went full ahead. This had the effect of swinging her bows back towards the pier instead of away from it. George and I took off at speed towards the shore. The tug smashed into the left-hand side almost bows on and, swaying violently, she cut through the timbers of the pier and very nearly severed the whole of the left side. The twelve by twelve timbers screamed as they were ripped apart and the tug came to a halt buried in the remains of the left head. To be honest I never found out for sure who was at the wheel that day, neither was it spoken about among the salvage men. The pier was quickly repaired, as were the bows of the sturdy tug boat. I did have a suspicion that Buncer was the man who was at the wheel and made the fatal mistake of going ahead instead of astern, but this has never been confirmed. I do know that shortly after that Mr Thomas asked my dad if he would consider taking over as captain of the 'Reeny' but Dad politely refused the post.

Buncer was still the mate of the tug when they were sent up to Port Glasgow on a job. As usual he spent his nights in the nearby pubs. One night he came back on board well and truly drunk but this was a night with a difference. The Luftwaffe launched a massive raid against the shipyards of Clydebank that night. The bombers came in vast numbers and began the total destruction of all below them. The main targets were further up the River Clyde than where the 'Reeny' lay moored. This mattered not to Buncer.

He climbed out of his bunk and onto the flying bridge where, taking hold of the Lewis gun mounted there, he began firing tracer bullets up into the blackness of the sky above the ship. For ages Buncer continued what he thought of as a one-man vendetta against the power of the German Air Force. At last the tug's ammunition finally ran out and Buncer crawled back to his bunk. The boat's only defence against an air attack was her Lewis gun and now there was nothing left to put in it. After that infamous episode, I did not see Buncer again until after the war, but I knew he had rejoined his old ship the *Fort Lennox* and was once more the bosun aboard her.

11

The Untamed

It was not long after my twelfth birthday, in the year 1943, when I was sitting at the front window of our house looking out over Port Bannatyne bay when I heard my father arrive, obviously in a great hurry. He began filling a large suitcase and called on my mum to help him. As they both filled the suitcase Dad explained to my mother what was happening.

'We have received a distress call from the Admiralty. It seems they have lost contact with a new submarine, which was training somewhere off Campbeltown. I have to be aboard the 'Reeny' in fifteen minutes.'

'Oh Attie,' said my mum, 'do you think the men will be all right?'

Dad slammed the suitcase shut. 'I don't know Mary, it will all depend on whether we can find her, what her problem is and most importantly what depth of water she's in.'

He hefted the suitcase, gave Mum a quick peck on the cheek, and charged down the stairs. We heard him open the bottom door and then he called up the stairs, 'Pray to God the weather stays as it is!' And he was gone.

I looked out the window again. I could see the 'Reeny' heading for the White Pier and a light lorry, filled with salvage men, travelling along Marine Road, also heading for the pier. The sun was setting and a reddish glow was spreading across the sky. The sea was calm with only the slightest ripple showing on its surface. I sat there, thinking about the men in that submarine. The idea of being trapped on the bottom filled me with a particular horror. I walked through into my bedroom and knelt down beside my bed. I prayed to God that night and asked him to let my dad find the missing submarine and save the men inside her. I remembered my dad's last words, as he left the house, and finished my prayer by saying, 'Please God let the weather stay calm exactly the same as today.' I lay awake for longer than usual that night, watching the darkening sky out of my bedroom window. I really felt the Lord had heard my prayer and my daddy would find that submarine and save the men in her. Here then is Dad's account of what happened.

When we arrived in the area designated for the search, there were two vessels already patrolling back and forth. One was the tug *Thrasher*, the other was the submarine training yacht *Shemara*, which had been involved in training exercises with the new submarine. The sub was one of the small 'P' boats and called the *Untamed*, with a dead weight of about 750 tons when dived and a crew of thirty-six officers and men. We were told the *Shemara* was fitted with the new asdics which she had deployed in her search. At first it seemed the *Shemara* might find her, for she picked up the sound of the sub blowing her tanks followed shortly after by the sound of the sub starting and stopping her engines. The *Shemara* had closed into the area, only to be greeted by silence. They had stopped the yacht's engines and tried tapping on their own hull, with no success. There was no answer.

Guided to an approximate area by the *Shemara*, the 'Reeny' began reading the bottom with her excellent French echo-sounder. This did not require audible sound as the *Shemara*'s asdics did.

We stood in the wheelhouse watching the trace, which was showing deep water and a gently undulating bottom. It was reading between thirty-three and thirty-five fathoms. It dawned on me that we appeared to be over an area of pretty level sand with no large rocks projecting above the bottom. I turned to our chief diver, Davy Bell. 'Is that bottom something similar to all around the Clyde estuary?' I asked.

'Yes, the Clyde is a huge estuary as you know Attie, and for millions of years the river has been belching silt and sand all around the isles of Arran, Bute and all the smaller isles. For the most part the bottom is pretty flat, similar to that.' He nodded at the trace moving over the graph. 'Why, what's on your mind?'

'I was just thinking, back home in Shetland we very seldom get such large areas of flattish seabed like that.' I pointed at the echo-sounder trace. 'There always seem to be jagged rocks sticking out high above the bottom, you would be surprised how many small boat anchors we lose when we're off fishing with hand lines back home.'

'What's on your mind, Attie?'

I thought for a moment, then said, 'Suppose we were to drop down a couple of small grappling irons, on about 250 feet of heaving line, do you think they would have a chance of skidding over a flat bottom like that without taking a grip?'

'Yes, I believe that could work. Not guaranteed of course, but it might work.'

'Fancy having a go at it?' I asked.

He considered for only a moment. 'I take it you mean trolling them behind the diving boat,' he remarked.

'Exactly,' I answered, 'we could cover extra ground by running a course parallel to the tug.'

'Why not?' Davy agreed. Let's give it a try.'

The diving boat was lashed alongside the 'Reeny', travelling with her as she searched the bottom, so the two divers, Peter Taylor and Davy Bell, and Danny McArra, the diving boat skipper and I, climbed aboard and slipped our mooring. Danny took up a parallel course to the 'Reeny', while I married two small grapnel hooks on a length of chain to 250 feet of heaving line. Davy was right, it worked fine, the hooks skidded over the bottom allowing the diving boat to travel at a decent rate without trying to pull her up.

For the next few hours we continued with our sweep. Occasionally the grapnel hooks gave a jerk as they bounced over some small obstructions, but because of the great depth, the heaving line was almost vertical and easily pulled the hooks free. Then suddenly the hooks took a real grip and the heaving line was sliding through my hands.

'Stop her Danny!' I called. 'Stop her and come astern.'

There was plenty of line left, coiled up in the bottom of the boat, but it was running out quite fast. I looked round anxiously at Danny. I need not have worried, Danny soon had her coming astern with a burst of power from the engine. Then, he eased her into slow astern and began skilfully steering her in the direction I was pointing. I began recovering the line until it was straight up and down.

'Stop her Danny!' I called loudly and with another short burst of power he stopped the boat dead in its tracks. My God that man could handle a motor launch.

I made fast the heaving line to the mooring posts on the stern of the boat and we signalled the 'Reeny' to come back to us. She did so, and passing slowly and carefully close by us, she confirmed we had a grip of something standing some twenty-five feet above the seabed. The rest of the diving team climbed down into the boat and I left them to it by returning on board the 'Reeny'. Davy Bell quickly dressed in his hard hat diving suit and prepared to make the dive. The tug's echo-sounder was reading 35 fathoms deep, beyond the normal limit for an air diver working for any length of time on the bottom.

The main trouble at such depths is nitrogen absorption of the body tissues, which causes a narcosis that divers call 'Rhapsody of the Deep'. Quite simply the human body becomes saturated with nitrogen, which initially produces the same result as being hopelessly drunk. Thereafter, if a diver surfaces too fast, he gets the bends. This condition can paralyse a man for life or even kill him, very quickly.

It is a strange fact that if a diver can remain sensible while consuming a vast amount of alcohol, off duty of course, then when he is sober, he is able to resist the effects of the narcosis better than a man who gets drunk easily. My two good friends Davy Bell and Peter Taylor both had a tremendous resistance to both the effects of alcohol and also nitrogen narcosis.

Davy stood on the diving ladder fully dressed, while his linesman attached a heavy-duty Seibe Gorman torch to the sidelight of his helmet. The linesman then screwed in the front light and with a tap of the hand on its top, he signalled the diver was clear to go. Davy took hold of the heaving line and slipped off the diving ladder. He descended as quickly as his ears would allow him to go, keeping his nose pressed against the bib inside the helmet. By blowing hard through his nose against the bib, he was continually equalising the increasing pressure in the Eustachian tubes between his ears.

The light began fading fast as he dropped, and every so often he would momentarily stop his descent by gripping hold of the heaving line and hanging there for a few seconds, to allow the diving pump to catch up with the continually increasing pressure. This was done by inflating the suit away from his body slightly, then once again he would slide on down. Above him, on the diving boat, his linesmen paid out the conjoined diving hose and telephone cable as he dropped. They listened to the exhaust air bubbling out of his helmet over the diver phone. By now Davy was studying the beam of his torch as it cut a swathe through the blackness below him. The water was exceptionally clear and the torchlight penetrated a long way down.

Davy slowed his descent when he observed a large shadowy shape emerging either side of his beam. He could now see the grappling irons below him.

'Bingo!' he said over the phone. 'It's the sub right enough, send me down a shackle on a light wire.'

When he reached the grappling irons, he found them hooked onto the submarine's jack stay at the rear of the conning tower. He climbed onto the conning tower to await the wire and shackle, and drawing a hammer out of his belt, he struck the access hatch several light blows which reverberated through his own helmet, like the ringing of a deep-throated bell. Then he listened intently. The silence that followed seemed the more intense after the sudden metallic clamour. Once again he struck the hatch, but this time he did so with more force. He smacked the side of the conning tower with a staccato barrage of eight blows and again paused. Other than the gurgling of his own exhaust air there was no response. The wire and shackle came sliding down the heaving line and after securing them to the jack stay, he freed the grappling irons. He then passed up the following information over the diver phone.

'The sub is lying at an angle of approximately twenty degrees, bows buried in a sandy bottom. Her stern well above the sea bed, she has no list and sits perfectly plumb. There are no indications of damage to her hull or conning tower. Most of her keel from the back of the conning tower to her stern is above the seabed level; this will make the positioning of lifting wires much easier. This also suggests she has blown her main ballast tanks but remains heavy forward of the conning tower. Possible flooding forward. All escape hatches are closed up and no sign of any attempt at escape can be seen. From a salvage point of view her condition is excellent, the main drawback is of course her depth.

'I'm getting pretty well narked up, so take up my lines. OK, I'm ready to stage off.'

His linesmen then prepared to decompress or 'stage off' their diver slowly to Siebe Gorman and Admiralty tables.

The following day we had the two lifting craft the LC8 and the LC9 positioned above the stricken submarine. In those days it was not possible to physically heave such huge dead weights to the surface. Instead we had to use tidal lift. This entails placing a series of heavy lifting wires under the vessel to be lifted and making them fast to the lifting craft on the surface above them. At the bottom of the tide, the wires would be heaved tight and spliced into loops around the bollards of the lifting craft by a team of riggers. Meanwhile, to give them more time to do their job, the lifting craft would slowly fill their tanks and settle down lower in the water to compensate for the incoming tide. Once all the wires were secured to the bollards, the lifting craft would pump out their tanks and this would bring every wire taut. They would then wait, while the rising tide would lift the sunken vessel off the bottom.

Next the tugs would take the lifting craft in tow, heading for some predetermined shallower water. The next tide would require all the wires to be shortened and spliced again and the same operation would be repeated until the vessel was brought ashore. In the case of the *Untamed* our team of divers placed thirty-six, three-inch diameter wires under her, all hanging from the LC8's bollards, then pulled back to the surface and spliced around the bollards of the LC9 by the team of riggers.

The lift went well and the submarine came off the bottom sweetly. The tugs took hold of the lifting craft and we set off, heading for shallower water. Unfortunately, the weather broke, the wind rose and the sea with it. The lifting craft began pitching and rolling, the heavy wires sawing at their specially-rounded decks. Mr Thomas was reluctant to call off the lift, as he still had hopes of finding some of the crew alive.

The wind and sea were obviously worsening as Mr Thomas and I stood on the bridge of the 'Reeny'. He finally turned to me saying, 'It's no use Arthur, we are putting everybody's lives in danger, the weather is getting steadily worse and there must be the better part of 800 tons hanging below us. I dare not take the chance that we could capsize the lifting craft.' He stood there with his head lowered, apparently looking at the heaving decks below us, then with a sigh he said, 'Cut her loose Arthur. It's hopeless, cut her loose and drop her back on the bottom.'

We dropped her back and the two lifting craft leapt upwards like two frightened horses. We had to abandon the lift as the bad weather worsened over the next few days so we were forced to make for the safe harbour anchorage of Campbeltown.

That first night Peter Taylor and I went ashore to have a drink in Campbeltown. We sat in a bar together, discussing all that had taken place. I remarked on the horror I felt at the thought of how these submariners had met their deaths and to my amazement Peter said, 'It's not as bad as you might think Attie.'

'How can you possibly say a thing like that?' I asked incredulously.

'Well,' 'Peter explained, 'if they all drowned to start with, then that's bad but it's a fairly quick death, because they would lose consciousness very quickly.'

'Yes' I answered, 'I see your point, but even the thought of drowning makes me shudder, and that's not what I meant. Davy reckons because of her buoyancy some of them must have survived in the dry.'

Peter took a long drink of his beer. 'I'm fairly certain a number of them must have survived for a while,' he said, 'but the point I'm making is, if they tried to escape from that depth, even wearing escape apparatus, they would have to flood up to equalise the pressure first. That means their bodies would be subjected to more than a hundred pounds per square inch pressure quickly. That would mean they would be narked to such an extent they would not care about anything.'

'Can it get you like that, really?' I asked.

'Get you like that? Honestly Attie, I've been so nitrogen drunk, I would have taken my whole helmet off, if I could have managed to get it off, because I believed I would still be all right without it.'

'Suppose some of them just waited for rescue instead of trying to escape?' I suggested.

Peter now agreed with me. 'Yes, I suppose that would be the worst scenario because their minds would be clear to start with, but carbon dioxide would soon cause them to fall asleep, a sleep from which they would never waken.'

On the way back to the ship that night, Peter explained a bit more about the so-called 'Rhapsody of the Deep'.

'There's a theory being investigated at the moment with regard to frogmen,' he said. 'Did you know, Attie, a frogman can go every bit as deep as we can, as long as he's supplied with air to the same pressure as we are, and yet they were continually being brought up without a mask, and dead. When one of them managed to survive, he explained he had experienced such a feeling of euphoria, that he was convinced he did not need any air sent down to him from the surface. He had decided he could swim like a fish and tore off his mask and threw it away. His diving mate, who was only slightly narked, grabbed him and taking a chance they both might perish with the bends he blew them both to the surface in a hurry. His mate saved the both of them, for luckily they did not take the dreaded bends.'

We walked along the pier towards our ship and I could not stop thinking about the men still inside that submarine.

Eventually the weather abated and we returned to our task, only now we knew there would be no survivors from the *Untamed*. It took us six weeks to get her ashore. The lads who opened her up had to wear special breathing masks. She emitted a foul gas, which was visible to the human eye. Once thoroughly vented, we entered her and found all her crew on board. Her fore-end had indeed been flooded, as Davy Bell had expected. The control room and engine room were dry, so again our knowledgeable chief diver had guessed correctly. In the bows of the submarine there was a sluice valve, which carried a clear warning that it must never be opened until certain procedures had been carried out: namely the closing off of either one or two nearby hatches. This was where the mistake was made. Human error was the cause of the tragedy – the wrong hatch had been opened first and due to the tremendous pressure of their depth, it had proved impossible to close it again. The boat filled so quickly the crew were unable to close off the first watertight bulkhead door.

Two men had made the attempt to pull it upwards using a small chain block. It is possible they only failed due to the boat going into a nose-dive to the bottom. There was evidence that the rest of the crew had survived for some time in the control room and engine room. Some of them were wearing Davis escape apparatus and one man had strapped two empty oil cans around his middle. Jack Duckworth picked up what he thought was a pair of light red gauntlet gloves, only to throw them down in horror when he realised he was looking at human skin complete with fingernails.

These men had indeed made a valiant attempt to blow their boat back to the surface. This had been confirmed by the *Shemara* reporting hearing her blowing her main ballast and for a while starting and stopping her engines to no avail. She was obviously far too heavy forward.

It was also proved that the remaining crew members had eventually attempted to escape by flooding the escape chambers of the engine room and conning tower, but never got the hatches open. As Peter had explained, they most probably succumbed to nitrogen narcosis, even though they were wearing Davis escape breathing apparatus.

To the present day, in the year 2008, I still have, in my possession, the two grappling irons which my father used to hook the submarine the *Untamed* sixty-five years ago.

12

SS British Commander

Uncle George Thomson was the youngest of my uncles. He was affectionately known as simply 'Geordie' by the family. In the year 1940 he was a merchant seaman on board the oil tanker the SS *British Commander*, sailing close to the island of Madagascar, in the Indian Ocean, when she was stopped by the German armed merchant ship the SS *Pinguin*, a ship specifically designed to prey on lone merchantmen and keep clear of convoys with their added threat of Royal Naval escorts.

The raider ordered them to abandon their ship and take to the lifeboats. The ship's radio officer made an attempt to send out a distress call for help, while the rest of the crew lowered the lifeboats. The warship opened fire and the ship's bridge and radio room were destroyed instantly, killing the radio officer. The warship approached silently and cautiously, as the merchant crewmen hurriedly left their ship and took to the lifeboats.

They were then ordered to come alongside the German ship and taken prisoner. Geordie would spend a good few weeks in custody down below decks. The German captain, however, was a very humane man and they were treated well. The captain had one particular penchant, which was to bring his prisoners on deck to witness the destruction of other British merchant ships he came across.

One day Geordie was brought on deck and saw a small steamer which was hove to and her crew were climbing into their lifeboats when a small gun on her stern fired a round at the raider. The shell fell into the sea well short of its target. The raider then blew the steamer out of the water and she sank in an incredibly short time. In the water were a number of men swimming for their lives and others clinging to carley floats. Now that the steamer was gone, the raider moved in to pick up survivors. Geordie saw a giant of a man swimming around and physically heaving much smaller men on to the life rafts.

When they were dragged on board he discovered the huge man was a Scottish Highlander and the little men were all Chinese. Some of the little men lay gasping on the deck but the bare-chested Scotsman stood bolt upright. His chest was running with blood from small shrapnel wounds. A German officer strode up to him and looking rather fierce he demanded, 'Who fired that gun?' The officer's English was impeccable.

The Scotsman towered over him and with a snarl he answered, 'How the bloody hell should I know?'

The officer decided to turn his attention to the small Chinese men, probably because they looked less intimidating. He marched up to one man, who was standing alone. 'You!' he said. 'Do you speak English?' The little man spread his hands and answered, 'No, I no speak the English.'

The officer made as if to turn away, then turned back and asked, 'Which of you Chinese speaks English?'

The little man spread his hands again, and shrugged his shoulders.

'I not sure, maybe you try number one fireman, maybe he speak the English.'

Geordie could not believe what he was witnessing. The officer ordered the Chinese crew to line up, still speaking in English, and they all moved quickly to form a line.

'Which one of you men is the number one fireman?' One man stepped forward. 'I number one fireman,' he said.

'Do you speak English?' the officer shouted at him.

'No sir, I no able to speak the English,' the man said. 'Maybe number two fireman speak the English.'

According to Geordie, it was at that moment that the German officer finally realised he was making a fool of himself and everybody was obeying his orders and all of them were speaking to him in reasonably good English. He began barking out orders in German and the German sailors quickly set up a machine-gun on the deck and trained it on the Chinese crew. The officer turned back to the lone Chinese man.

'You tell me who fired that gun or I shoot your shipmates!' he shouted loudly.

'You let me ask them please,' the man said.

The officer appeared to calm down considerably. 'Right, you go and ask them,' he answered.

There seemed to be quite a long discussion between the Chinese sailors before the man returned to the officer. 'Nobody know who fire gun,' he said. 'You let me join others please, before you shoot.'

A commanding voice, speaking in German over a loud-hailer, interrupted the fiasco. The German sailors jumped to remove the machine-gun and a very subdued German officer quietly told all the prisoners that they were once again ordered to go below decks.

The prisoners' quarters were steadily becoming overcrowded and the heat was barely bearable but the food was good and plentiful and they had access to their own fresh water, the latter being the most important thing due to their latitude in the Indian

Ocean. Geordie believed the warship's captain felt a certain sympathy towards merchant seamen and wherever possible he appeared to try and lessen the harshness of their plight. In this respect, he stood alone, for Geordie never ran across his like again. In fact Geordie would later report such incredible hatred from Germans, in all walks of life, towards the English-speaking nations, that it was almost unbelievable.

In the words of the German innkeeper in 1938, the Germans had prepared well. A raider is only effective if it is supplied with fuel to search for its quarry, with ammunition to destroy that quarry, with food and vital supplies for its crew and a safe place to receive them. A predetermined meeting place had been arranged between the battleship and its supply ship. A raider feels safe on the high seas, whereas in close waters it still fears the might of the Royal Navy, the prime sea power at that time. The *Altmark* was that supply ship and she lay waiting for the battleship in the vast expanse of the Indian Ocean.

Wireless communication was forbidden, so they must find each other by seamanship alone. The battleship duly arrived and began taking on fuel and ammunition. The transfer of prisoners then began, and lastly stores and provisions were taken on board. The German ships were highly efficient and all was completed in the shortest possible time with both ships still sailing in close proximity abreast of each other. Geordie would later grudgingly admit that the German seamanship was superb.

The *Altmark* was already carrying prisoners, taken previously, and the new arrivals found themselves condemned to a life of hell, permanently below decks. They were to find they were on starvation rations and worse than that, fresh water was also rationed. Geordie was luckier than most – at twenty-one years of age he was on the plump side to begin with, so he had considerably more reserves to fall back on. As the weeks went by, the

Altmark crammed more prisoners into her holds, as she serviced several raiders, such as the *Graf Spee*, the *Gneisenau*, the *Pinguin* (alias the *Kormoran*) and the *Kormorant*.

Conditions deteriorated rapidly below decks and the prisoners' general health began to break down. Geordie was by now suffering acute starvation and his condition was aggravated by the lack of sufficient fresh water, which might have alleviated the swift decline. By the time the *Altmark* ran the gauntlet of the Royal Navy to land her prisoners, to be despatched to Germany, most of them were more dead than alive.

German guards rounded up the emaciated men and they began the long march through Switzerland and into Germany. Men who fell by the wayside were beaten back to their feet and forced to carry on marching. It was on this march that Geordie first met Leslie Harris, a Canadian sailor. Almost at the end of his tether, Geordie decided he had had enough. Three prisoners had mysteriously disappeared, and it was rumoured the guards had shot them and left their bodies in the woods. Nevertheless, Geordie slumped to the ground, determined he could go no further. Before the guards could reach him, he was grabbed by Leslie Harris and hauled back onto his feet. The tall Canadian swung one arm around Geordie and half dragging him, he marched on. Geordie swore from that day onwards that Leslie saved his life. He was certain that the guards would have killed him, when he was unable to rise any more.

At last they came to the prisoner of war camp Stalag 8, *Milag und Marlag Nord* (Merchant and Royal Navy North). This was to be their home for the duration of the war. All this had taken place in the early years of the war and for a time the prisoners were reasonably well treated and their rations, though frugal, were such as allowed a partial recovery from the dire treatment they had received to begin with.

They were set to work on the German farms around the camp and Geordie would experience the terrible hatred that Hitler had instilled in the German people as a whole nation. They were kicked and spat upon and vilified, every time they left the camp. The guards did nothing to stop the abuse their prisoners were having to endure.

At home, Geordie had been posted as missing for a considerable period of time and his mother, old Granny Thomson, was out of her head with worry for her youngest son. We were all so relieved when a small postcard arrived telling her Geordie was alive and well and was a prisoner of war in Germany.

In his next letter to his mother, Geordie said he was working every day on farms near to their camp. One day one of Granny Thomson's neighbours, Alice Dewar, stopped her in the street saying, 'Oh! I am so happy for you Bella, I have just heard Geordie is a prisoner of the Germans and he is fine.'

Our old granny came into our house and said to our mum, 'You know Mary I don't think Alice Dewar understands the concept of world war.'

'How come?' our mother asked.

'Well, when I told her the Germans had Geordie working on their farms, do you know what she said?'

'No, what did she say?'

'She said, Oh! That's fine Bella, so you will be all right for eggs from now on.'

The years rolled on, and as the war began to turn against Germany, so the treatment of the prisoners became harsher. The camp guards were still confident that Germany would win in the end. One day Geordie and Leslie were on latrine duty in the camp. This consisted of pulling a large square box, lined internally with lead and mounted on wheels, around the camp and emptying the noxious contents of the camp's dry toilets into it, for disposal in a large hole dug in a nearby field. As they pulled the cart past two of the guards, one guard called out in German, 'One day we have Winston Churchill pulling that cart.'

To which Geordie replied in fluent German by lifting one hand up to the level of his own neck and saying, 'Yes and Hitler will be in it, up to here.'

He was dragged away and severely beaten, stripped naked and placed in a circle drawn in the snow outside the huts. He was told if he stepped outside the circle he would be shot. For almost two hours Geordie crouched shivering in the snow. The camp inmates had been informed by Leslie what had taken place. They began one of the noisiest demonstrations ever heard in a prisoner of war camp. This forced the guards to relent and they carried Geordie to his hut and threw him inside, throwing his clothes in after him. Only the menacing rifles kept back the angry hordes of prisoners.

'For God's sake man why do you antagonise the bastards like that?' said Leslie.

'Because that's what they are,' Geordie croaked. 'A bunch of fucking bastards and some day, some day . . .' He collapsed shivering on his bunk.

Slowly but surely the deterioration set in. The prisoners were now becoming emaciated. The daily rations had been cut so often over the past year that every man in the camp could think of nothing but food, all day and every day. Gone were the days when they would smuggle a potato or two into the camp and use the peelings to make a rough brew of alcohol. Then they had the occasional skins of the fruit supplied by the Red Cross to add to its flavour and potency. Now there was nothing, no Red Cross parcels, no potatoes, no skins even, of fruit of any kind.

At last came the morning when Geordie stood before a mirror lathering his face, in preparation to shave himself. He raised the cut-throat razor to his side laps and it hung there as he studied his reflection in the mirror. The gaunt face looking back at him was grey and lined. The narrow shoulders were painfully thin and they had a permanent hunched-forward look. His breast-bone jutted forward against the stretched skin of his chest; it was altogether too much. With horror Geordie realised he was contemplating swiftly drawing the razor across his own throat and putting an end to it there and then. He swore later that he would have, had he not noticed a movement in the mirror beyond the open washroom door behind him. A large, well-fed farm tabby cat had climbed through the barbed wire and was trotting towards the washroom. Geordie turned away from the mirror and reaching the open door, he called loudly, 'Here kitty kitty, here kitty kitty,' in German. The farm cat came trustingly. From that day onwards and for the rest of his life my uncle could not stand the sight of a pet cat, although he admitted killing and eating the animal had saved him from taking his own life.

When the Allies liberated the camp, Les and Geordie pleaded with them to be given guns but the soldiers refused at first. They had driven their tanks straight through the barbed wire fences to allow the foot soldiers the quickest entry. The camp guards had left a matter of a few hours beforehand. They were unlucky as they tried to run deeper into Germany. They ran straight into Allied soldiers who had executed a pincer movement around the camp in anticipation of just such a move by the Germans. They were herded up and brought back to the camp. At the sight of them the ex-prisoners had to be forcefully restrained from a mass attack on the hated men.

The Allied troops were horrified at the condition of the seamen and the whole camp in general. They found the overall treatment of the prisoners had not been so much removed from concentration camp standards. Geordie and Les continued to beg for rifles and ammunition. They now had the full sympathy of the disgusted soldiers and were given a Lee Enfield rifle each. Nothing, however, would induce the troops to give them any bullets for the guns. What they did do, was allow Les and Geordie to march away with the most vicious guard of all. This was the man who had taunted Geordie with the latrine cart and beaten him senseless and left him naked in the snow. He now marched before them with arms raised above his head. He could not know the two rifles menacing him were empty. He was taken to a small quadrangle the Germans had used for special punishments, over the previous three years. Some of the men who had survived these special punishments had described to their fellow prisoners the inhuman treatment they had received. Some men were taken there and never seen again.

The German was made to run back and forth between them. He was beaten with the rifle butts as he did so, like the prisoners were over the years. The hours passed and the German's strength ebbed away. He was now crawling on all fours, dragging an obviously broken leg.

The hardened resolve of the two seamen allowed no room for sympathy toward the German. Over their years of captivity, they had listened to so many stories of this man's cruelty. They had also waited in vain for comrades who did not return to describe what had happened to them.

The German was screaming for mercy and could go no further, when they left him to the ministrations of the liberating army. Now they felt they were free to leave that accursed place. They took the road to freedom and carrying their empty rifles, they headed back the way the liberating army had come.

They passed some of the farms they had been forced to work on. The German owners came out, pleading with them to write out notices in English to say they had been well treated there, and to spare their farms from destruction. Geordie was so angry, remembering what these people had done to them, but he smil-ingly agreed to do as they asked. The Germans produced large cardboard placards and thick black crayons. Geordie and Les set to work telling the passing forces how they had suffered there as POWs and would they please oblige by throwing all the furni-ture out of the windows of the farmhouse without opening them first. They felt a certain poetic justice as they accepted the heart-felt thanks from the German owners, before going on their way.

Geordie arrived home and was advised he would be hospitalised to begin with. The powers that be wished to make an early attempt to repair his body and his mind. He would eventually marry one of his nurses. She was a sweet and gentle-natured girl from Kent, the Garden of England. She became my Aunt Marjorie, the youngest of my aunts. Firstly, Geordie came home to Scotland to see his mother, old Granny Thomson, and since she was living with us in Port Bannatyne, we were the first of the family to welcome him home. The war was still dragging on and the port was full of Royal Navy men.

One early evening Geordie walked into Charlie Walker's inn and asked for a pint of beer. He stood at the bar and directly behind him, sitting around a table, were four Royal Navy sailors in uniform. One of the sailors noticed the small circular Merchant Navy badge Geordie wore in his lapel. Nudging one of his mates and smiling broadly the man said loudly, 'Merchant Navy man, is that what you are?'

'That's right.'

'And have you seen much of the war up to now?'

'As much as I ever want to.'

'Oh! As much as you ever want to,' said the sailor, smirking at his mates. 'What were you on, a big ship maybe, say, the Isle of Arran ferry?'

'What are you?' Geordie asked. 'Besides being a smart bastard.'

The smile vanished off the Navy man's face. 'Watch it buddy,' he said rising from his chair, 'I might just have you outside.'

'Don't call me "Buddy",' said Geordie in a menacing tone. 'And let's go outside right now.'

The Navy man looked uncertain but tried to bluff it out.

'You might need some help,' he said, 'there are four of us here.'

'Hang about,' said Geordie, 'I'll be right back,' and he shot out the door. He came straight upstairs and told my dad what was happening. Dad and I were sitting eating our lunch. Dad shoved himself away from the table and stood up. 'Let's go,' he said. Geordie entered the inn first, followed by my dad, who stood just inside the door and said loudly, 'My brother-in-law here has something to sort out with one of you guys and everybody else is going to sit quietly and drink their beer.' He then folded his massive arms across his fifty-six-inch chest, openly displaying his number twelve shovel hands. Dad was a big, big man, weighing sixteen and a half stone of solid packed muscle at that time and in nature he was as hard as nails.

The apologies came thick and fast and the smart Alec of the group was thoroughly ashamed of himself when he learned that Geordie had just returned after spending more than four and a half years in a German prisoner of war camp.

13

The Andrea Doria

In the summer of 1958 I was diving with the firm of Balfour Beattie, who had a contract to re-line the intake and output tunnels which supplied the cooling water for Portobello Power Station's turbines. There were three of us hard hat divers employed to caulk the clutches of the coffer dam which lay approximately a quarter of a mile off from Portobello beach. The three were Sandy McGill from Leith, Leslie Doe from Australia and myself from Edinburgh. Both Sandy and Leslie were much older men than I was and I believe that Leslie left me alone because of my comparative youth, but my God he tormented Big Sandy almost daily. He was the ultimate joker in the pack and most annoyingly he would laugh heartily at his own wild antics.

We would go down in the early morning and take one side each of the dam to caulk with Denso Cord. This was necessary to reduce the amount of water being forced into the dam under the pressure of the sea outside. While Sandy and I would work away conscientiously, it seemed Leslie became quickly bored by the mundane repetitiveness of the work, which admittedly continued day after day, with monotonous regularity, but at the same time, it was very well paid work.

On the seabed we each had an iron ladder, which allowed us

to clamber up and continue caulking to a much higher level. Every two feet we progressed up from the sea bed reduced the pressure of the water by approximately one pound per square inch. Thereafter we would climb on to a staging, lowered from the surface and controlled manually by the men above us on the timber gantries. They would set the staging to suit the level we wished to work at. In this fashion, we could plug leaks up to thirty feet above the bottom, thereby reducing the water pressure by approximately fifteen pounds per square inch.

Sandy might be kneeling on the bottom working away and Leslie would crawl round to Sandy's side and creep up behind him and smash the top of his helmet with his caulking hammer. He would then hit his chin switch and Sandy and I would hear his maniacal laughter roaring into our helmets via the diver phone. Sandy would hit his own chin switch and say, 'For God's sake man, give over before you punch a hole through my helmet.' Leslie would chin his switch again, 'That's the trouble with you Scots, no sense of humour.' Followed once more by his hellish laughter.

The chin switch, or 'buzzer' as we called it, lay just inside the right rim of the helmet and when activated, a little light lit up on the console on the diving boat accompanied by an aggressive 'brrrr' to draw attention and identify the diver communicating. It operated as a relay system, so only one diver could speak at a time. On the boat of course, the linesmen and boatman would hear everything that went on inside our helmets as we would alternately chin the switch to have our say.

If Sandy happened to be up on his iron ladder caulking to a higher level, then Leslie would climb up behind him and ram the handle of his caulking hammer up Sandy's bottom and none too gently either. Sandy would tell me later, 'It's more the fright I get when the bastard does things like that, that's what bothers me, more than anything else.'

Sometimes Leslie would just grab Sandy from behind and press in Sandy's spindle valve. He would hold on doggedly while Sandy fought to get clear, with his suit inflating steadily and threatening to blow him to the surface.

Leslie Doe was a big man, not tall, around five foot nine, but with a fifty-six inch chest, brawny arms and a thick-set body, this made him a big man. He had dived all over the world, he told us, adding and many other places. In the Persian Gulf, working for an oil company he went down one day and landed on the back of a large manta ray. She had babies under her wings and promptly turned up her spear of a tail and rammed it through his standard diving suit, through the right side of his belly and out through the left side of his belly and then through the suit again. When she sped away, luckily the tail broke off and Leslie was hauled aboard the diving boat.

He was flown to Guy's Hospital in London, still wearing the suit and with the manta ray's tail untouched by anyone. The surgeons cut the suit off him in the operating theatre, before cutting Leslie open to remove the manta's tail. He reckoned that was what saved his life. He showed us the scars of the two puncture holes on either side of his vast belly and the mass of stitches, which ran right up its centre The doctors told him he was a lucky man – he had a ruptured spleen and lost part of his liver and with the overall damage to his subcutaneous tissues he would never dive again. This news was greeted by his usual roar of raucous laughter as he told them, 'I have never done anything other than dive all my life and I will continue to do so until I depart this life.'

Big Sandy and I became the best of mates and would continue diving together for many years. Sandy was six feet tall with a forty-four inch chest and the heaviest legs I ever saw on any man. He also had a great temperament and the most infectious laugh to go with it. Large also in the eyes. They sparkled with merriment and shone with a deer-like sheen when he had a drink or two in him. We sat in a bar one evening talking about the Aussie and Sandy said, 'Bobby he's a head case, look at the dents in the top of my helmet, what normal man carries on like that?'

'To be honest Sandy I'm glad he leaves me alone, for I would chin him if he did that to me. However having said that, I still admire you for not punching him.'

'The only thing that stops me is the thought that he is really mental and God knows what he might do to get his own back. I tell you Bobby, I'm sure he is a head case.'

Our attention was drawn to the news on a television set above us, as a newscaster reported the death of another American skin diver, diving on the wreck of the *Andrea Doria*, an Italian liner which sank in 1956 after a collision with a Swedish ship called the *Stockholm*, which had ice-breaker bows. The liner had gone down off the city of Boston, on the eastern seaboard of the USA.

Three days later, Leslie Doe told us he was leaving. Some very rich people had contacted him and asked if he was willing to dive the *Andrea Doria*. It seemed their lives had been saved by the *Stockholm*, but their precious jewellery had gone to the bottom with the liner. So we waved goodbye and normality returned to the job. The only men who were sad at his leaving were the linesmen and the boatman, for they had heard everything that took place on the bottom, via the diver phone, and they had found it great entertainment.

The previous summer of 1957 we had completed the last of the three small intake tunnels and also built the wooden gantries and piers around the larger outfall tunnel, which was still in operation and delivering beautifully warm chlorinated water, which was a delight to swim in. We had a heavy mooring rope strung across the centre of its powerful wash, at surface level, to prevent us from being swept away. We would hang onto the rope during lunch breaks and enjoy the most forceful and luxurious jacuzzi you could ever imagine.

On the gantries, the riggers had built a Henderson sheer leg steam crane with its 120-foot high jib. This was then used to pitch and drive the Larsson steel piles of the square coffer dam around the mouth of the shaft on the seabed, that led down to the outfall tunnel, 110 feet below the sea. We left four piles out, one in each corner, to allow the tide to ebb and flow inside the dam, without putting pressure on it, and we left it like that over the winter months.

Now it was the summer of 1958 and with the final four piles driven and the dam de-watered to seabed level, Sandy and I felt like the painters of the Forth Railway Bridge with a job that never ends. We would complete the caulking of the clutches and the slightest storm would crush the Denso cord to the thickness of a razor blade. Then with the pressure coming off with the calm weather the dam would leak heavily once more. It was true there was a battery of pumps inside the dam, but to allow them to cope we had to continue caulking to ease down the water ingress.

We would arrive for work in the early morning inside the power station yard along with our linesmen, boatman, the concrete squad, labourers, shuttering joiners and pumpmen. Only the pumpmen, divers and linesmen would climb aboard a large amphibian DKW or 'duck' as we called it, for we would go out to the job by sea. All the rest of the men would go down seventy-five feet in a lift to the eight-foot diameter tunnel (now dry) and set about their work of lining the walls with fresh concrete. Our boatman, Eddie Ponton, would jump up into the duck's driving seat and with a deep-throated roar he would gun the powerful engine into life.

We would travel slowly out of the station and down onto the sandy beach, and one lovely summer's day, while we still had Leslie Doe with us, we were rolling down over the sand and passed two young women in swim suits sunbathing. When Leslie sang out, 'Hold on Eddie, hold on for a minute cobber' Eddie stopped the duck and Leslie leaned over the side and said to the girls, 'Hi girls! Fancy coming out to the dam with us, out there you will get a far better tan than you will here.'

One girl sat up and said, 'Hey you are Australian yes?' Leslie was obviously taken aback.

'Too true, don't tell me you're both Sheilas.'

It turned out the girls were indeed Australian nurses and trustingly they climbed aboard the duck and we rolled on down to the sea and into it, engaged the propeller and we were off. As we sailed out to the dam, I caught myself thinking about the men who originally built these tunnels, seventy-five feet under the sand, more than fifty years before. They were what we divers called 'Tunnel Tigers' and like us they worked in compressed air. Unlike us they had very little knowledge of the properties of compressed air and the dangers attendant upon it. They were usually lured by the big money that was always on offer.

When we arrived at the dam, the duck was moored on the sunny side, to suit the young nurses, but rather than sunbathe, they were more interested in watching us get ready to dive. Firstly our linesmen dressed us in our Siebe Gorman woollens, two pairs of thick short socks, two pairs of thigh-length socks, two pairs of long johns, two jerseys and finally a red woollen hat. Next a canvas cummerbund went around our middle, pulled tight by three buckles. There is a popular misconception regarding all the woollens. It is true they keep us warm, but more importantly, they prevent the suit from sudden wrinkling with pressure changes and gripping areas of skin in a vice-like grip. Usually the lower legs were all right but from the knees up everything was vulnerable, almost to the waist.

Very often a man would scream in pain when a wrinkle would snap over like the spring of a rat trap in a place where a woman would be completely unconcerned. You had to very quickly inflate by pressing in your spindle valve and blow the wrinkle out.

The flamboyant Leslie was holding all the attention of the two stunning girls. He sat down and the linesmen began drawing the suit up his legs. The taller of the two girls reached out and gripped the top of the suit. 'Oh! It's like canvas,' she said.

'That's what it is honey,' said Leslie. 'It's made from alternate layers of twill canvas and thin rubber sheets bonded together.'

'Is it very heavy?' the smaller brunette asked.

'Not once I'm in the water it ain't,' Leslie said as he stood up. The linesmen gathered around him and gripping hold of the bib they began the fight to get his fifty-six inch chest inside. It seemed more of a struggle today but then their eyes kept flicking over the two swimsuited nurses. The tall girl wore a one-piece suit cut low at the back which covered her breasts without going over her shoulders. The other, smaller, girl wore a black bikini.

In the suit now, Leslie sat down and placed his feet into the deep diving boots, secured by three buckles and also heavy sash cord bound tightly around the legs immediately above the boots. It would never do to lose your boots while on the bottom, the air would rush down and inflate your legs and very quickly turn you upside down and send you bulleting to the surface completely out of control.

'Gosh!' the big girl said. 'These look heavy.' She bent over and lifted one of Sandy's boots. 'Oh my god,' she exclaimed, obviously struggling with the weight. 'How do you manage to walk with these on?'

'Diving is a man's job,' said Leslie with a smirk. He omitted to tell the girl that the boots weigh very little once you're under water.

The corselet was passed over his head and the six holes in the suit's rubber top were fitted over the stud bolts of the corselet. Two at the bottom front, two at the bottom back and one on each shoulder. The brass bands were now fitted over the bolts and the linesmen screwed them down tightly. They passed a broad leather belt around his middle, which had a built in brass holster in which lay a Siebe Gorman heavy-duty diving knife.

'How would you get out of that in an emergency?' the small brunette asked.

Leslie was enjoying every minute of the attention he was getting from the girls. 'It's the best and safest gear in the world,' he said, standing up. 'One thing is for sure though, my darling, no man will ever get out of this gear by himself be he in the water or out of it.'

His linesman secured a safety line around his middle and Leslie walked over to the diving ladder and passed the loop of the safety line over the ladder stringer. The big girl followed him saying wistfully, 'Oh! How I wish I could come down with you.'

Leslie turned back towards her and bending forwards, he held onto the rim of the corselet with both hands and pretended he could pull it away from his body. 'Jump in then and come down with me,' he said.

'Could I?' the stupid girl said eagerly, even though she had witnessed the struggle it had taken three linesmen and a boatman just to get Leslie into the gear.

Leslie laughed, backed through the stringers and stepped down the first two rungs. Now his boots were in the sea. Here he was at his most vulnerable, if he should fall off the ladder and the safety line break, then without a helmet he was a dead man. His linesman placed two very heavy lead weights, one on his chest and one on his back, and tied them around his waist. Next he lifted on the helmet and passed the telephone cable under Leslie's left arm and secured it to his left window. His air hose was passed under his right arm and tied to his right window.

Three feet from his helmet both lines came together and were bound to form one manageable line for easy coiling. Lastly his linesman screwed in the front light and gave it a final tighten with a tommy bar across its two studs. He handed Leslie the shot line, which was made fast to the ladder – the other end was on the bottom tied to a weight. This was the vehicle that would take Leslie to his job. His linesman signified he was clear to go by slapping the top of his helmet. For the benefit of the girls, Leslie made a spectacular backwards leap off the ladder, bounced back to the surface amidst a welter of foam and bubbles and sank slowly out of sight. How that man loved to show off.

'Oh!' the big girl said, 'I'm going down with him.' She dived over the side into the bubbles erupting from Leslie's helmet. She arrived back on the surface within a minute. 'Oh! It's really deep out here,' she gasped as she climbed up the diving ladder. She came out the water naked from the waist up. The dive in had turned the top half of her suit downwards. She stood on the deck and using both hands swept her long hair back and began squeezing the water out of it.

All male eyes were goggling at the girl's exposed breasts when the little brunette said quietly. 'You've come out of the top of your swimsuit.'

Only then did the big girl realise what had happened. 'Oops!' she exclaimed. 'Sorry about that,' and she promptly whipped up the front part of her suit. 'We're all sorry now,' said Eddie Ponton, putting on a forlorn face. The girl favoured him with a shy smile.

One morning shortly after Leslie had gone off to America, Sandy and I were dressing for the day's work when a message came through telling us to motor across the River Forth to Kircaldy harbour. We were told another hard hat diver was trapped against the sluice of the main harbour gates and we were to go to his aid. We had actually set off when we were given an immediate recall. It transpired that Royal Naval divers had arrived on the scene.

That evening we were to find out that the diver was James Ward, a very good friend of Sandy. It had taken the Navy divers two hours to get him clear of the sluice and by that time it was too late, Jimmy was dead. This man was one of the finest divers who ever came from the British Isles. He was a stonemason by trade and had gone all through the war tackling the most hazardous jobs, sometimes jobs that other divers had turned down.

One such job was the removal of a block ship from a French harbour; Jimmy was cutting it up into sizeable pieces using under-water burning gear. The retreating Germans had booby-trapped the ship but instead of cutting between the ship's frames, which is the easiest way to go, Jimmy was cutting on the frames them-selves – a much longer and more awkward job. The Germans had set their high explosive charges dead centre between the frames. If Jimmy had been cutting there he would have been blown sky high.

After the war, Jimmy was employed by the Leith Docks Commission, as second diver to Martin Bendicks. His main work was laying the new blockwork of the Albert passageway and maintaining all the stonework on the dock bottom. On that fateful day, it was Jimmy who was sent to Kircaldy to remove an obstruction to the gates, a job which had always belonged to Martin Bendicks. Such is the strange way fate sometimes works. This was a routine job that Martin had carried out a hundred times over the years, in all of the small ports in the Forth estuary and yet on that day, for some inexplicable reason, it was James Ward who was sent for the very first time. A veteran diver of many years then lost his life due to that unexplained change of routine procedure.

14

The Deep Diving Record

I have every reason to remember 1960 well. From the very outset things had been going wrong. The main outfall tunnel was virtually complete and the diving work was temporarily suspended. Jo Cowan had made me up to night shift foreman until such time as the diving resumed. I had the use of his office during the night. My duties were simple enough: each night I clocked all the men in at 8 p.m., and saw all the concrete squad and labourers go down the lift shaft into the tunnel to their work. At the same time Eddie Ponton would rev up the duck and take all the pumpmen out to the coffer dam to man the pumps. I would complete the nightly sheets and around midnight would go down in the lift and walk through the tunnel towards the coffer dam.

The first three hundred yards were complete, so I was alone as I walked through. The tunnel was very well lit with literally hundreds of bulbs strung all the way along. In the brightness of their light, the new concrete walls were impressive in their smoothness. At the far seaward end, I could hear the noise of the compressors running and soon came upon the first of the labourers working behind the concrete squad. I would continue past the squads until I came to the shaft up to the seabed. Here we had an eighty-foot long Larsson pile standing at an angle from the shaft bottom to the top. It had steel rungs welded across its clutches every nine inches. I would then climb up the makeshift ladder and arrive at the seabed. From there I had another four smaller ladders to climb before reaching the working platform on top of the dam. Up here were the controls for the battery of pumps that kept the seabed comparatively dry.

The seabed could take about three feet of water before any would spill down the shaft and into the tunnel, but no more than that. The workmen's huts also stood on the platform and were equipped with gas cookers and heaters for the comfort of the men. I would now climb over the top of the dam and down again to reach the duck. Eddie would be waiting there to run me back ashore. I would repeat the whole routine again around 3 a.m. or sometimes about 4 a.m. The idea was to keep the men on their toes and prevent them from falling asleep in the early hours.

I arrived one night feeling really unwell and by the time I had clocked all the men in, and seen them off to their work, I knew I was not going to complete a twelve-hour shift. I sat in Jo Cowan's office and my head was going down by the minute. I thought, if I can just hang on until the local pubs shut at 10 p.m. Unfortunately I only lasted until 9 p.m. and was forced to tell our messenger to run me home and not let anyone know I was not on the job. The following day I was tucked up in bed with a raging flu and Mabel walked in to my bedroom with the foreman from our job, big Willie McFarlane.

'Hi! Bob,' the big man said in his Glasgow drawl, 'how are you feeling?'

'Not very good at the moment Willie,' I answered. We made small talk for a few minutes, then Willie sprang it on me. 'They let you down, you know,' he said.

'Don't tell me,' I answered. 'What's happened, nobody hurt I hope?'

'No, but there could easily have been some of them killed. As soon as you left, all the pumpmen came back ashore and into the Battery Bar. They drank there until ten and then came away with a carry-out that would have paralysed a horse carrying it. They had a party on the coffer dam and, blazing drunk, they fell asleep. The pumps ran out of fuel and stopped. The coffer dam filled to the brim, as did the shaft and the tunnel.'

'What about the squads in the tunnel?' I asked.

'Oh! They had to get out in a hurry but they said it wasn't flooding terribly fast to begin with, but it built up in speed later.'

'Did nobody phone out to the dam?'

'They tried to, but got no answer and the duck was alongside the dam the whole time so they couldn't get out there.'

'How did it finish up?' I asked, desperate to know the final outcome of this disaster.

'When they woke up they started all the pumps but since the dam had lost all pressure every clutch was pouring in and they were making very little headway, but the stupid buggers didn't tell us when we arrived and your big mate Sandy and the first lot of the day-shift boys climbed into the lift and started off down. The roars from the men when they hit the water alerted the winchman and he brought them straight back up, like a bunch of drowned rats. Do you know what Sandy said to me coming out of that lift with the water pouring off him?'

'No,' I said, 'but I can imagine he wouldn't be very pleased.'

Strangely enough Willie was smiling. 'He said, "What are you trying to do to me? Are you trying to get me to beat the deep diving record without a helmet?"'

Fully recovered from my bout of flu, Sandy and I were back to caulking the clutches of the dam once more. I now had a new linesman, a tall, broad-shouldered young Canadian called Simon Le Croix. While he was training he taught me a bit of a lesson.

My telephone had been acting up so I sent it ashore to be fixed and decided to carry on working with hand signals – after all, sealing a dam is pretty basic stuff. I was standing on the ladder ready to go down, while Simon tightened my front light. This done, a linesman is supposed to place the shot line in the diver's hand and tap him on the helmet as clear to go. Simon placed a rope in my hand, tapped the helmet and I backed off the ladder. I floated for a few seconds as usual, then started down. I tried to slow my descent by hanging onto the so-called shot line, then, pulling on it, I discovered I had hold of a short length of rope about six feet long made fast to nothing.

I knew instantly I was in deep trouble and slammed my spindle valve shut but I was still accelerating downwards. Inadvertently I called out. 'Catch me Simon!' but of course I had no phone. Now I was really motoring down and the air in my suit was being compressed so quickly I had no buoyancy at all. The suit gripped my body as it began its inexorable crushing pressure, a thousand times more powerful than an anaconda. The diving pump couldn't save me, it couldn't catch up with that rate of fall. I felt my ribcage start crushing and my ears screamed out their pain in my brain. Another ten feet and I was dead. I was suddenly jerked to a halt and the diving pump began easing that terrible pressure. Only my ears continued to scream at the abuse they were being subjected to. I hung there for about six or seven seconds, just enough time to inflate my suit away from my tortured body, and I was off again. My lines were falling free once more. As fate or luck would have it I slammed into the bottom after another fifteen feet of fall.

Now I was in a quandary. I was safe from being crushed to death but my ears felt as if four-inch-long nails were being driven into them. What should I do? I dared not spindle up, in case I got the dreaded reverse ears. This condition could burst my eardrums and possibly flood my Eustachian tubes with mucous, thus rendering my middle ear useless and leaving me suffering from Eustachian catarrh. As luck would have it, as I pondered the situation, my ears hissed out a partial equalisation and I decided to climb up my own lines to the surface. This I did, being careful to remain slightly on the negative buoyancy side all the way up.

After stripping down to my woollens, I sat trying to recover in the cabin of the duck. I knew I had survived an experience which could easily have killed me. Young Simon did not realise the seriousness of what had happened. We went through the comedy of errors as they happened.

1. The spare piece of rope had been one of a few Simon had cut to splice rope grommets to make a doormat. He had laid it on the gunnel of the duck beside the shot line which, as always, was secured to the stringer of the diving ladder.
2. I did not check the rope was secure before stepping backwards off the ladder.
3. I had no phone to warn Simon I was in free-fall.
4. Simon had watched my coiled lines flowing over the side unconcernedly. He did say later, 'I did think you were going down much faster than usual.'
5. When a double coil jammed across the diving ladder stringers and jerked me to a halt fifteen feet from the bottom, Simon had been frantically trying to free it. I thank God he didn't manage it too quickly.

We all sat drinking a cup of tea in the cabin of the duck and discussed the near-tragedy. I was taking very shallow breaths because of my bruised ribcage. I told Simon about Lieutenant Commander Peter Keebles' excellent book called *Ordeal by Water* in which he tells the story of the divers cutting off the damaged propeller of the battleship *Vanguard* after an attack by Italian frogmen. One diver fell off the staging slung under the ship and plunged down forty feet. His linesmen were unable to prevent his fall because his lines were around the bulging underwater torpedo protection.

His body was crushed up into his helmet with such force that when the helmet was brought to the surface and the linesmen automatically unscrewed the front light, nothing came out but a reddish ooze.

Simon asked, 'Why was that, if he only dropped forty feet?'

'It's the first forty feet that's the most dangerous for a standard suit diver,' I started to explain. 'Any given volume of air is exactly halved at approximately thirty-three feet deep.'

'What does that mean?' Simon asked, 'in ordinary terms that an ordinary guy might understand.'

I thought for a minute, then said, 'Suppose I take a pint glass tumbler and turn it upside down and place it carefully on the surface of the sea, all the air is trapped inside and as I sink to the bottom with it and the pressure increases the water is forced up inside the glass. At thirty-three feet it equals one atmosphere, fourteen point seven five pounds per square inch and inside the glass the water level has risen exactly halfway, so the volume of air has been halved. If I take it down to sixty-six feet it will be halved again, but since there was only a half at thirty-three feet then at sixty-six feet there's only a quarter of the volume left. So you see, the quick squeeze comes from the surface down to forty feet or critical weight of eighteen pounds per square inch. If a diver is down over a hundred feet and falls forty he can survive; he'll be bruised but he can survive. But he won't survive a free fall of forty feet from the surface down. His body, bones and all, will be crushed upwards into his helmet, which is incompressible.'

116

Simon's mouth drooped open as he struggled to follow my explanation. 'You mean I could have killed you.'

'You certainly could have,' Sandy said. 'If Bobby's lines hadn't fouled up on the diving ladder, he would have been crushed to death. When I was training in the Navy they taught us that diving is not dangerous, until you forget that it can be.'

'My fault to begin with,' I conceded. 'I didn't check the so-called shot line was secure before stepping off the ladder.' I was trying to ease the young Canadian's guilt. 'However, all's well that ends well. Like Sandy a fortnight ago, I thought I was going for the quickest deep diving record.'

Young Simon smiled at my joke, then said, 'Oh! By the way, I see Jacques Picard has just broken the deep diving record.'

Now this was something I had been interested in all my life. 'I never heard,' I said, 'how deep did he go this time?'

'Down to the bottom of the Mariana Trench,' said Simon.

'Don't be stupid,' I found myself saying. 'Last year he went down three and a half miles in his bathysphere. That's only half the depth of the Mariana Trench.'

'Well,' said Simon, 'I don't know about that, but he has done it.'

'Don't talk nonsense Simon,' I said. 'Have you any idea how much weight there would be in a wire rope more than seven miles long. To say nothing about a pressure in excess of nine tons per square inch.'

The young man shook his head. 'Again, I don't know about all these things,' he said. 'But he has just done it, and I'll bet you thirty shillings that he has.'

'I've a good mind to take the money off you,' I said, 'just to teach you a lesson.'

'I'll hold the stakes,' Sandy said cheerfully.

Simon dug one hand in his pocket and began counting out

thirty shillings. I did the same, saying to Sandy as I did so, 'I'm going to take the money off him to teach him a lesson.'

Sandy gathered up the cash and pocketed it with a smile. 'One of you is going to be very sorry,' he said. 'This is a hell of an amount of cash to lose on a bet.'

The following day Simon came on board carrying a magazine that told the story of Picard's greatest discovery. He had introduced a brand new technology to the deep diving scene. The bathysphere had been relegated and in its place he had invented the bathyscaphe, a small submarine called the *Trieste*. This amazing little craft had only a half bubble protruding from its underside in which Picard's son and a lieutenant from the US Navy made the dive. The rest of the submarine consisted of individual tanks filled with kerosene and open to the sea at their bottoms. The thinking was brilliant. Kerosene is lighter than sea water and at the same time, as it is almost impossible to compress a liquid, there could be no pressure exerted on the little craft. Only the bubble had been constructed to withstand the colossal pressure of the deepest part of the earth's oceans. I conceded that Simon had won the bet and in return he made me a present of the magazine. A sixpenny magazine cost me thirty shillings.

15

Of Crooks and Comic Singers

Shortly after the unfortunate flooding of the dam and tunnel, at the time I had come down with the flu, I was sitting in Jo Cowan's office filling in the time sheets and making out my nightshift report. It was just after 2.30 a.m. and all the men were down below in the tunnel, working away. In the power station yard, where I was, all was quiet and dark. It was with difficulty I finished my report up to that time for the stillness was getting to me and I could feel myself getting drowsy. To prevent myself from falling asleep, I walked through to the little washroom and splashed my face with cold water. I was towelling my face dry when a knock came on the office door.

'Come in,' I called loudly, walking back into the main office.

The door opened and two very tall men came in. They were both dressed in white gabardine raincoats and there was something about them that suggested authority to me. Instantly I was on my guard.

'What can I do for you gentlemen?' I enquired politely.

The taller of the two flipped open a wallet briefly.

'CID,' he said.

'Oh!' I said. 'Take a seat lads, is there something I should know about?'

They both ignored my suggestion to be seated. The taller of

the two said, 'We are looking for escaped prisoners from Saughton prison. We understand you have quite a few Tunnel Tigers working down below.'

'We have quite a few men working down below, but they're not Tunnel Tigers,' I said. 'The tunnel is at atmospheric pressure and relatively dry.'

'Whatever,' he grunted, loudly and irritably. 'We would like to have a look at them, can you take us through the tunnel?'

'You want to go now?' I asked. 'Or can I offer you a cup of coffee first?' I was only observing the pleasantries we always extended to any notable visitors to the job.

'We want to go *now*,' said the previously silent one. I got the impression they were worried I might have some means of communicating with the men and might warn them about their coming.

'Right,' I said, pulling on my duffel coat. 'Let's go.'

When we reached the lift shaft, the first detective turned and in little more than a whisper he said to me, 'On the way through the tunnel, we don't want you to speak to anyone at all, got that? Not one word to anyone down there.'

'As you wish,' I said, and we descended in the lift. At the bottom we stepped out and I said, 'These railway sleepers go all the way to the far end, so if you step from sleeper to sleeper, between these rails, we will pass through the centre of the men.'

'What are the rails for?' one of the men asked – for the first time in a normal voice.

'We have a large circular shutter which travels along on the rails,' I answered. 'You'll see it, at the far end when we get there.'

We walked on in silence and the noise from the far end began to increase.

'What makes that racket?' one of them asked.

'That's the labourers using jack hammers to smash out the old

12 Commercial Street, Lerwick, Shetland, 1933

Grandad Sinclair and the Author, aged 2 years.

Salvasen's SS *Coronda* formerly SS *Politician*.

Strain Hall Church as Evacuees' Primary School, 1942.

Port Bannatyne, Isle of Bute.
Back row from centre to the right Mr J R Stewart, Michael Morgan, David Steel, the Author, George McEwan.
Front row, 7th from left, my sister, Isobel Sinclair.

Geordie – Proud to be a Scotsman.

Geordie seated second from the left.

Prisoners' cartoons: escape attempts

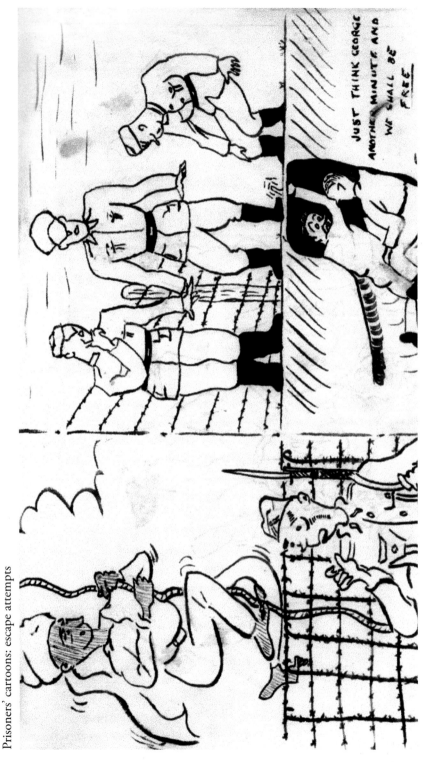

Prisoners' cartoons: home brew

W. T. Seal M/V British Union
sunk by German Raider Command.
18th Jan. 1941

CORNWALL ENGLAND

James. A. Croll captured By
Admiral Scheer. Dec 18. 1940

Ex. T.S.S. Duquesa

SCOTLAND

DUNDEE No. 12

William, Charles, Alfred. Bettis (Desolate the one and only)
R. Commander.

Sunk By Pinguin.
27 Aug. 1940.

LONDON

Monty Walker (Smith) — 3   (EDINBURGH)

S. S. "Craftsman"

Sunk by Raider "Cormoren"
S. Atlantic 4th April 1941

EDGWARE. MIDDLESEX.

Leonard Williams,   Sunk 24/11/40.
Admiral Von Scheer.

M. V. Port Hobart.

LONDON

James Hughes
S/S Mopan Sunk by the Admiral Scheer
November 5. 1940
Liverpool 8

Prisoners' details and their ships

JOSEPH. WALLACE
S/S. MOPAN.
SUNK BY ADMIRAL SCHEER
5/11/40
LANCASHIRE LIVERPOOL

Harry Healy
SS. Orama sunk by Von Hipes
8-6-40
LONDON

William. E. Andrews, Ship Cook S.S.S. Duquesa, South
atlantic, Admiral Scheer, 18/12/40,
117 Rhodesia Road
Liverpool 9.

William. Cooper, Chief Cook.
Capt. Hobart
43 Woodman Street North Woolwich
London E.16

Norman Wharton
S/S Mopan
Sank by Admiral Scheer
5/11/40 Liverpool. 8

Malachy Malin   M.V. "British Strength"
155 London Road   15 - 3 - 41.
Grays Essex.

John Mullen Sunk June 1940
36 Hamilton Road
Bellshill
Lanarkshire Scotland

Prisoners' details and their ships

PORT. WELLINGTON.	24:11:40.	AUSTROUS.	22:2:41.
TRIBESMAN.	1·12:40	TRELAWNEY ·	22:4:41.
TRIONA.	6·12:40	MALKSEAH	24·2·41.
TRIADIC.	8·12:40	GOR DUFF.	7·3·41.
TRIASTER.	8:12:40	ATHOL. FOAM.	15·3·41
ANASTASIA	18:12:40	BRITISH STAR.	15:5:41
DOGRSA.	18·12:40	POLYCAMP.	15:3:41
ANTONIS.	6·1·40	SAN. CASIMOIR	15:3·41
BRITISH. UNION.	14·1·40	CHILEAN REEFER.	16:3:41
CARAVELT.	20·1:40	DEMETERION.	16:3:41
STAN PARK.	24·1·41	EMPIRE INDUSTRY.	16:3:41
MANDASOR.	29·1·41	GRANLI	16:3:41
TRI STAR.	29:1:41	SILVER. FIR	16:3:41
LYCHOCHUS.	31·1·41	SIMNIA	16:3:41
SPEY BANK.	5:2:41	SARDINIAN PRINCE.	16:3:41
ANGULARITY.	11:2·41	ANNTA	22:3:41.
ICELAND.	22:2·41	BRITANIC.	25·3·41.
BRITISH. ADVOCATE	20:2·41	CANADOLITE.	25:3:41
KANDION CRUISER.	21:2·41	SR. ERNEST. CASSEL.	4:4:41
KANTARA.	22:2·41	VOLTAIR.	4·4·41
TED HUFF.	22:2·41	CRAFTSMAN	9·4·41
HARLESDEN.	22·2·41	RHE REIVER	11·4·41

Ships represented in the Prison

GahDew.	24 : 9 : 39		King. John.	13 : 7 : 40
Frieda Morn	28 : 9 : 39.		G.Racefeilo.	14 : 7 : 40
Brot	18 : 10 : 39		Wendover	16 : 7 : 40
Rawahpindi	23 : 11 : 39		Eypenia Albanoi	24 : 7 40
Shie.	21 : 10 : 39		Domingo De.haronaya.	31 : 7 : 40
histhe Brae.	9 : 4 : 40		Kilhonay	10 : 8 : 40
ahmonpooh.	3 : 5 : 40		Turakena	20 : 8 : 40
cientest.	3 : 5 : 40		Kassel.Hohn.	25 : 8 : 40
Saherno.	3 : 5 : 40		British. fame.	12 : 8 : 40
hoek.	12 : 5 : 40		British. Commander.	24 : 8 : 40
sesjelnt.	23 : 5 : 40		huminach.	4 : 9 : 40
Oil.Pioner.	5 : 6 : 40		Bymbehing.	3 : 9 : 40
Orama.	8 : 6 : 40		Athel.King.	7 : 9 : 40.
VanDyke.	3 : 6 : 40		Bendvam.	6 : 10 : 40.
hady. of Man.	13 : 6 : 40		Natia.	8 : 10 : 40.
hitish. Petrol.	13 : 6 : 40		Mofan.	5 : 11 : 40.
hawfehh.	11 : 7 : 40		Teddy.	11 : 11 : 40.
harmatten.	1 : 7 : 40		Nowshera.	18 : 11 : 40
hhambre.	4 : 7 : 40		Maimoa.	20 : 11 : 40
hanreit.	1 : 7 : 40		Port. Brisbane.	21 : 11 : 40
Davisian	10 : 7 : 40		Port. Hohbert.	24 : 11 : 40
Mahpap.	11 : 7 : 40		Rangitani.	26 : 11 : 40

Ships represented in the Prison

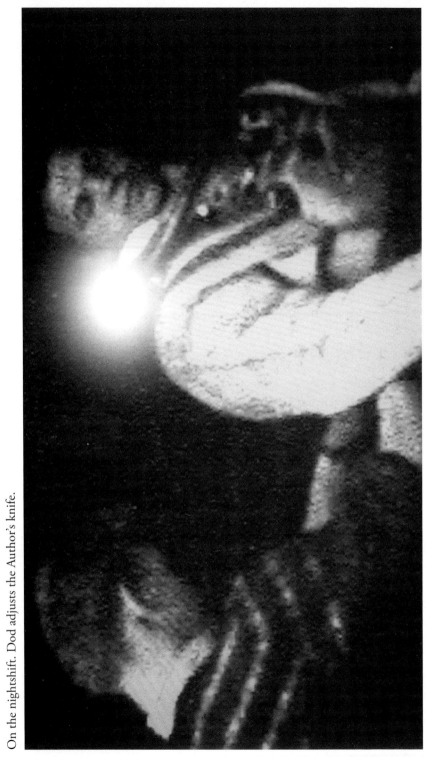

On the nightshift. Dod adjusts the Author's knife.

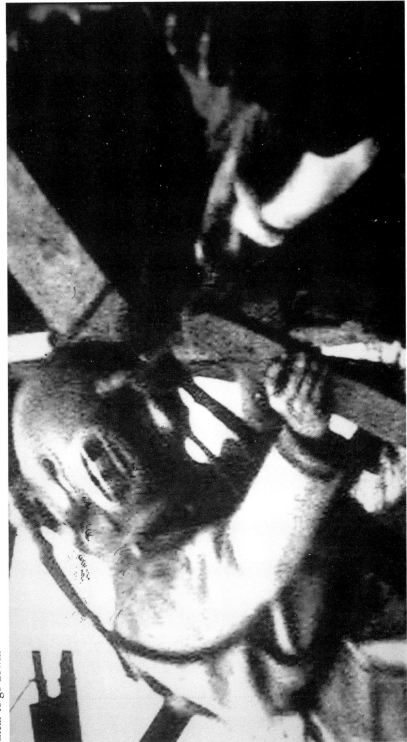

Clear to go down.

East end of Cockenzie Bay as the Dam (in the background) heads into the sea.

L-R: Martin Bendicks, George Smiles, The Author. *Reproduced by kind permission of The Scotsman Publications.*

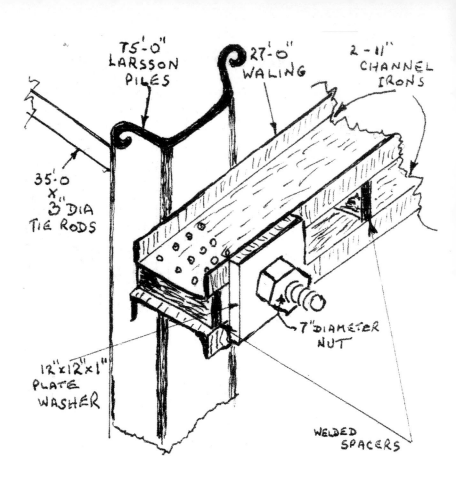

75'-0"
LARSSON
PILES

27'-0"
WALING

2 - 11"
CHANNEL
IRONS

35'-0
X
3" DIA
TIE RODS

7" DIAMETER
NUT

12"x12"x1"
PLATE
WASHER

WELDED
SPACERS

Sketch of walings
and tie rods

concrete ahead of the concrete squad, replacing it with the new,' I answered.

Once again we walked on in silence until the taller man said, 'We would prefer not to come back this way, if it is possible, after we have seen who is down here.'

'That will be no problem,' I said. 'I make my rounds twice every night and I come this way, and return by boat to the shore.'

Once again we walked on in silence until the men up ahead came in sight and the same detective warned me again. 'Remember, not one word as we go past them.'

We got some strange looks from the men as we passed by. I felt sure they had recognised the detectives for what they were. We came to the bulk of the circular shutter, fully expanded, and it forced us to squeeze our way between it and the shuttered tunnel wall and carry on to the seaward shaft. I noticed a change in the two detectives' attitude as they stood looking up the height of the shaft. Gone was the arrogant superiority they had shown up to then, and in its place was obvious concern over the vertical climb ahead of them. I honestly believe they would rather have turned back if they could have done so without losing face. I stepped between them and started to climb the pile ladder. They were forced into following me.

Reaching the seabed, I almost laughed out loud at their concerned look up at the height of the coffer dam still standing above us. Two months later my own father must have had similar thoughts of misgiving, when faced with the same challenge, although he had not shown it. He was an old man, while they were in their prime. At that time I never considered that we were all young men ourselves and were used to working at height; they were not, and that does make a difference. We climbed up and over, and down again to the timber gantry, where the duck lay moored and I cleared my throat noisily to awaken Eddie, asleep in the driving seat.

All the way ashore we sat in silence and when we reached my office I once more made the offer of a cup of coffee. They both declined in a gruff manner and made as if to leave me and walk towards their car.

'Wait a minute fellows,' I called after them. 'You're surely not going to leave me without telling me whether or not you saw anyone you knew down there?'

They both turned to face me and spoke in turn. The first said, 'Your job is full of crooks and comic singers.' His tone of voice told me he really meant it.

The other detective said sarcastically, 'The only person missing down there is Ali Baba himself.'

The following shift I found I was two men short among the labourers in the tunnel. I heard later that Eddie Murphy and little Jake Millar had again taken up their previous residence in Saughton prison.

16

The Medical

It was not long after the tragic death of James Ward in Kircaldy harbour and we were still working at Portobello power station on the outfall tunnel. The old boom defence ship the *Recovery* arrived carrying a new demountable circular shutter which was to replace the old one. Unfortunately, the sling gave way as the Henderson derrick transferred the shutter to the timber gantry. The individual components, being banana-shaped, scattered far and wide when they landed in the sea. I was given the job of retrieving them. This meant searching the bottom over a wide area and gathering the individual pieces together in one place, so they could be loaded on a rock pan lowered to the bottom by the derrick.

I would load so many then allow the derrick to take them up, while I gathered some more for the next lift. In between times, I had to wait for the return of the rock pan to the bottom. On the gantry, Sandy McGill was supervising the lowering of the rock pan into the shaft inside the coffer dam. This meant a considerable period of time would elapse before the return of the rock pan to me on the seabed. I was lying against an inclined rock face and waiting patiently for the return of the derrick when I noticed a medium-sized crab squeezing a small mussel between his pincers. He kept turning the mussel around and squeezing it, then turning it around and squeezing it again. The mussel finally gave up and cracked open. The crab settled back on his hind legs and using both pincers began tearing the flesh of the mussel and feeding voraciously. He was stuffing the meat into his mouth so violently that small pieces of meat began drifting upwards above the crab. As if by magic a school of codling appeared and began swooping down and eagerly swallowing the free meal. The crab went berserk and, dropping the mussel, he strove with all his might to reach up with both pincers and fight off the freeloaders. The fish easily evaded his clumsy antics. He gave up and, lifting the mussel once more, resumed his violent feeding with the same result. More and more codling arrived and by the time the rock pan slammed into the bottom again, the crab was literally foaming at the mouth. By the time I finished my job, my undersea friend was going absolutely mad with an insensate rage consuming him. I left him trying to climb up the inclined rock face I had been resting on, with the misguided idea that the extra height was all he needed to catch the robbing swine.

Sandy came on the diver phone the moment the last of the shutter left the bottom on the rock pan. 'Come up,' he said, 'Jo Cowan wants to see us.'

'What does he want?' I asked.

'I don't know, the message came out from the shore just now.'

I clambered aboard the duck, stripped off and we were soon speeding towards the shore. Mr Joseph Cowan was Balfour Beattie's agent. He was the man in charge of the whole job.

When we arrived at his office and entered we found that Mr Thomas Black, the SSEB clerk of works, was also present.

'Both of you have to go for a medical tomorrow,' Jo said.

'Why's that?' I asked.

'Because there's been a change in the law,' he answered. 'You have to go before a specially selected diving doctor and he must certify you are fit enough to continue diving.'

'And what happens if he says we are not fit enough?' Sandy asked.

'Your diving days are over,' Jo replied. 'It has just been declared as the law in the UK and all companies must obey.'

'You lads have nothing to worry about,' said Tom Black cheerfully. 'Now do you want the good news?'

'I'm always happy with good news,' I said, 'so fire away.'

'Tell them Jo,' said Tom.

'Our company is tendering for a brand-new power station, which requires an awful amount of diving work and Tom and I are putting your names forward for the underwater work,' Jo said.

'Provided we pass the doctor,' said Sandy.

Jo Cowan spread his hands. 'We can't do anything about that,' he said.

'Och,' Tom said, 'you young fellows are as fit as fiddles, you'll pass all right.'

Jo picked up a paper from his desk and handed it to Sandy. 'You both have an appointment to see Dr Gordon Batters tomorrow morning at ten o'clock in Constitution Street, Leith.'

The following morning, Sandy and I were sitting in the doctor's waiting room at the appointed time. His nurse told us I would be the first to see him, followed by Sandy. We both had learned this first meeting would determine whether or not we would be issued with a diver's 'Fitness Register', which in its turn had to be written up and signed by the doctor every three months, before we would be allowed to carry on working as divers.

Naturally this caused quite a bit of trepidation in the two of us. We had been together for almost three years and had just heard the good news we were being considered for a new power station to be built on the sea. The practice nurse called, 'Mr Robert Sinclair?' and I was ushered into the doctor's surgery. The nurse introduced me to Dr Gordon Batters and left the room.

The doctor was a very small, slimly-built man in late middle age. I towered over him. He had very wispy light brown hair struggling valiantly to cover an almost bald pate. He appeared to be very worried as he said, 'Take a seat young man,' and walked around his desk.

'I did not ask for this you know,' he confided in me. 'It's been thrust upon me, because of this.' He sat down and indicated a model of a Royal Naval destroyer which lay upon his desk. 'I was a lieutenant in the Navy,' he continued morosely, 'but that was many, many moons ago.' He lifted a pen, studied its tip intently, then continued as if he was ready to burst into tears.

'You will have to help me,' he said. 'I can't remember what critical weight is, in diving.'

'Critical weight is eighteen pounds per square inch pressure and is equal to forty feet of sea water,' I answered.

'Oh! Thank you,' he said, and began writing on a notepad. He drew a large ledger forward, studied it, and for the first time his face cleared. 'So,' he said 'You were a petty officer in the Navy yourself? What ships were you on?'

'I was never on a surface ship,' I replied. 'I was only National Service and spent most of my time training. Basic at Victoria Barracks Portsmouth, underwater damage control, Dolphin 2 submarine base, firefighting at Phoenix, ABCW warfare, then HMS *Royal Arthur* petty officers' training school and on to a Royal Naval airfield, HMS *Nuthatch* at Anthorn on the Solway firth.'

Now the medical began, every bit as extensive as my days in the Royal Navy. Eyes, ears, nose and mouth, chest and lungs, blood sample, urine sample, blood pressure and chest X-ray. He put me through it, and finished at last. He presented me with my first Fitness Register duly signed. He also told me I was the first diver in Scotland to own one.

I hung around waiting for Sandy and at first all was peaceful and quiet. A sudden raising of voices from the doc's surgery suggested things were not going so good for Sandy. The door opened and they both appeared, the doc looking really worried once more.

'Your blood pressure is very high,' said the doc.

'Every diver gets high blood pressure!' Sandy almost shouted at the doc. 'Diving gives everybody high blood pressure, that's not the point!' he continued, getting louder. 'I could dae it in ma baries!' By now he was shouting.

The poor doc turned to me saying, 'What is he saying? What does he mean, for God's sake, what does he mean, what does "dae it in ma baries" mean?'

I tried some calm words to soothe him, saying quietly, 'He means we are not working at extreme depths and he could do it in his bare feet.'

I was not prepared for the doc's response – he burst out laughing and had to sit down because he was hurting himself with laughter. It was infectious and before we realised it we were all laughing our heads off, even the nurse had joined in. The doc reluctantly gave in afterwards and signed Sandy's Fitness Register but not before saying first, 'Remember it is not only your own life that is at risk but also your fellow divers in an emergency.'

Sandy, however, had the last word as we left the doc's premises, as he said, 'If a man lives long enough doc, you can be sure he will die.'

17

Cockenzie Generating Station

We had some time to wait before the SSEB inspected the finished outfall tunnel at Portobello. All the men had been paid off except the shore liftman, the pumpmen on the dam, Eddie Ponton, the duck driver, Sandy and me. I was once again doing my night shift as foreman. One night I was having a drink in the Kingscross bar with my father, prior to going on the night shift. I was telling Dad about the tunnel, how it was constructed and such, when he said. 'I would have liked to have seen that.'

I said, 'Would you like to see it now?'

'Could I see it now?'

'Certainly. It's only six o' clock and I don't start until eight. Come on, I'll take you through the tunnel and bring you back by sea.'

We left the bar and walked down to the power station. I called the shore liftman to drop us down and he did so. Dad said nothing as we walked through the deserted tunnel, now eerily silent but still brilliantly lit. He stopped and looked at me. 'How far are we under the sand at the moment?' he asked.

'Approximately seventy feet,' I said.

He said nothing but shook his head as if marvelling at the thought. When we reached the seaward shaft, he stood looking up at the circle of lights around the top of the shaft seventy-five feet above us.

I indicated we now had to climb the pile ladder and without a word Dad set off, with me climbing behind him. Arriving on the seabed, he stared up at the cluster lamps all around the head of the dam. We then climbed to the top and over and down again to the duck. Eddie ran us ashore and Dad said nothing until we were back in the bar. He then let his breath out with a whoosh and said, 'What are you trying to do to your Dad? Don't you realise I'm nearly sixty years old?'

'I never thought of that, you being an old sailor I thought you'd be used to going aloft, especially since Shetlanders like yourself are supposed to make the best seamen at climbing the rigging.'

'Aye, but that was thirty or forty years ago.'

Shortly after the work was completed at Portobello and Balfour Beattie had cleaned up and left I received a letter from Tom Black saying he wished to see Sandy and me in his office at Portobello. We were greeted warmly by the jovial big man, who had once confessed to both of us he wished he had tried the diving when he was a younger man. He had the drawings of the proposed new power station at Cockenzie laid out on his work bench and he drew our attention to them.

'I'm afraid Balfour didn't get the contract as we had hoped,' he explained. 'Instead it went to the Mitchell Construction Company.'

'So,' I said, 'I take it we've lost the chance of the underwater work?'

'Not a bit of it,' he said with a laugh. 'That's why I sent for you. I told Mitchells' agent Eric Hume that he should sign the two of you on, as you are both very experienced divers. He admitted to me he had no experience of this kind of work, so I agreed to help him recruit the type of men he would need, such as piling foremen and gangs, general labourers and such like. And you two to look after the underwater work.'

'Thanks very much Tom, that was very good of you,' Sandy said.

'It was my pleasure lads,' said Tom, pulling forward one of the drawings on his bench.

'George Wimpey did all the test bores of Cockenzie bay and here are the results.'

Sandy motioned me forward, while he stood back. He had confided in me years before that as a young boy he had suffered from Bright's disease and, unable to attend school, he had never learned to read or write.

'Ah!' I said, deliberately out loud for Sandy's benefit. 'What have we here?' And I bent over the drawing.

'Max depth of water approx fifty feet to a sand bottom. Depth of sand approx fifteen to twenty feet on top of fairly level brown sandstone rock.' Tom Black placed a second drawing on top of the survey vessel's report I had just looked at.

'Oh my God,' I exclaimed. 'You're intending to reclaim the whole bay from Preston Links colliery to the old Cockenzie harbour.'

'Told you didn't I?' Tom said triumphantly. 'The biggest diving job you will ever be on.' He tossed a third drawing on top of the others. 'There you are, the biggest dam you will ever work on.'

I took one look and again exclaimed, 'Wow, two lines of heavy duty Larsson piles in parallel but thirty-three feet apart overall.'

I winked at Sandy secretly and cupped an ear, as if listening. 'Three-inch diameter tie rods, thirty-five feet long bolting both sets of piles together. One rod on the seabed, one rod in midwater and one rod above the surface, every five piles. The finished piles to be infilled with red blaize gravel to a level above the highest spring tide, all the way.'

I was really impressed by what I was looking at, although I

pretended I was in such awe of the job that it had caused me to describe everything in detail. The main thing was that Sandy now had the full picture.

That evening we both sat in my local bar, the Speedway Arms, discussing the days events.

'These tie rods you described will have to go through holes burned in the piles after they're driven,' Sandy said.

'That's right, I agree, but the rods are only three-inch diameter and they're asking for five-inch diameter holes. That gives us a little leeway for pitching them.'

We were talking as if we already had the job.

'Are you happy using burning gear?' Sandy asked.

'Certainly,' I answered, 'why, have you got a problem?'

'I haven't burned anything underwater since I went through my training at HMS *Vernon* in 1943.'

'What did they teach you to use?' I asked.

'A Seafire torch,' Sandy replied.

'Have you never used oxy-arc burning gear?'

'No, never.'

'Don't worry about it Sandy, I'll have you burning with it in no time. By the way, who was your instructor at HMS *Vernon*?'

'It was a petty officer diver called Sam Stanley.'

'Did you ever meet his wife Mary?'

Sandy showed surprise. 'As a matter of fact I did, Sam took Martin Bendicks and me to his home to meet her, did you know her?'

'I never met Stan or Mary,' I replied, 'but Mary is my wife Mabel's cousin.'

'It's a small world,' said Sandy.

'When we go for this interview Tom Black has set up with the guy Eric Hume, if he wants me to read anything, I've left my glasses at home,' he then said determinedly.

'No problem Sandy,' I said in agreement.

At the actual meeting, we discovered not only was the agent a comparatively young man in his late thirties, not a great deal older than myself at thirty-one, and much younger than Sandy at forty-three, but he had a refreshing honesty about him. He straightaway made us aware that he had no knowledge of piling or diving and was anxious to surround himself with men who were experienced in that form of construction.

'I've signed up two piling foremen this morning,' he said. 'Perhaps you might know them? Martin Donleavy and John Bruce.'

Sandy and I laughed and Sandy said, 'Manhole Heid and Old Brass. We know them well and they're damn good men.'

The agent nodded saying, 'Tom Black sent them to me and I've left it up to them to recruit their own men. I also have to purchase something called "A" frames and "flying frames" for them to work with.'

'Bobby and I will make the A-frames,' Sandy said. 'You'll only have to buy the timbers. The flying frames come later, when we reach the sea.'

'You seem to know the work well,' Eric said.

'I should, I'm a shipwright to trade, with years of experience of piling,' Sandy answered.

Eric turned to me and said, 'Are you the same?'

'No,' I answered, 'I'm a ship's joiner.'

Eric's brow wrinkled, 'What's that?' he asked.

'A shipwright with his brains bashed in,' I said, and Sandy laughed aloud but Eric gave only a weak smile.

'I understand I may require as many as ten divers to get the work done in the time I'm required to complete it,' he said.

'You only require the two of us to start with,' I said. 'Then build up as we go out to sea.'

133

Eric turned to Sandy. 'Will you take the chief diver's job for me?' he asked.

Sandy noisily sucked in his breath and shook his head. 'Bobby here is the man you want for your chief diver believe me.' He made a point of emphasising the 'believe me'.

Eric seemed surprised at Sandy's refusal but he immediately offered the job to me and I accepted. 'Now,' he said, gathering in a large diary lying on his desk. 'You will have to let me know what equipment I need to bring in for the underwater work. I want to have everything on site beforehand, so there's no delay in getting started.'

Now he was talking like the agents we were used to.

'Can I make a suggestion of how I see the job starting off?' I asked.

'By all means.'

'Well, Big Tommy Black showed Sandy and I the drawings for the job, starting from the west side and the proposed site of your temporary offices on that side. So to begin with Sandy and I will take off all the materials we will need for the A-frames and build them. At the same time we'll erect the offices, when they arrive. It will probably take a few weeks before the dam progresses down the beach and into the sea and that will give us time to assemble the diving gear in a shore hut, prior to our getting a diving boat.'

'Yes,' said Eric, interrupting me, 'but I have to know what diving gear I have to order for you.'

'I was just coming to that,' I said. 'Balfour were so sure they would get the contract that they had assembled all the diving gear in readiness, all except boats. They even had brand-new diving helmets, still in their packing cases, oxy-arc underwater burning gear and welding torches. Now, rather than have all that expensive gear lying in storage sheds, doing nothing, don't you

134

think a shrewd agent from another construction company could negotiate a mutually agreeable hire rate for the whole lot?'

I knew I had hit all the right notes by Eric's reaction. 'Do you think they'll agree to hire it all to us?' he said hopefully.

'I'm sure of it,' I replied. 'A dam such as we are going to build here is a one-off job, one they lost out on, but a hire rate will help them defray some of the cost of all that equipment they bought for it.'

'Do you know who I should get in touch with?' Eric asked.

'I think you should have a word with Tom Black, he and Jo Cowan had a better relationship than any other agent and clerk of works I ever met,' I said. 'Now, we need to consider where we're going to get a diving boat from.'

18

Diving Boats and Cowboy Divers

We had taken delivery of a new fibreglass hull, of the type used as a deep-sea liner's lifeboat, built by Weatherheads' small boat-yard at the old Cockenzie harbour. The bare hull had an inbuilt Lister diesel marine engine, open to the elements to begin with. We soon had her decked out and a cabin fitted forward; the stern was reserved for the use of two divers and their linesmen. Amidships there was a shelf to take the diver phone and a seat beside it for the boatman to attend the phone. She was named the *Tom Eadie* after the famous Dundee hard hat diver who had saved Winchester cathedral from settlement, which was threatening to break it up.

Eric Hume had purchased a second boat called the *Otter*. She was an ex-harbour pilot's launch with a Kelvin diesel engine. She too was quickly converted into an acceptable diving boat. I had started my cousin George (Dod) Donaldson and a mate of his Ian Crow as trainee linesmen and also my old uncle Buncer as a boatman. They would make up the crew of the *Tom Eadie*. The problem was getting divers. We were advertising all over and I was having to give up diving time to interview everyone who answered the adverts. I knew it annoyed Eric, me in the offices instead of underwater, but he refused to take the interviews himself so what could I do? He was one of the best agents

I ever worked for but he was also one who pushed hard for his company. He wanted me to start some of the cowboys who were turning up but I was reluctant to do so. I felt I would never be able to live with myself if one of them managed to kill himself on a job where I was the chief diver. Many a time I would be on the bottom with Sandy, who by this time was using oxy-arc like a veteran. I would be pitching tie rods through the holes Sandy was burning ahead of me and Dod would come on the phone. 'You've to come up,' he would say in a lazy drawl.

'What's happening?' I would ask.

'Another interview with a so-called diver.' His tone of voice suggested absolute disgust, after all, he had been privy to so many similar messages with no end result. Sandy, of course, would also hear the message and chin his switch and say, 'Here we go again, I'm handcuffed to a ghost, now I have to burn the holes and pitch the tie rods as well, why don't you stick a broom up my bum and I'll sweep the seabed for you at the same time.'

There was no real animosity with Sandy, it was just his sense of humour.

One day after a similar call, I walked into my office and found a young man waiting there for me. He said his name was Jerry O'Hara and he was wearing a well-tailored sports jacket and over its breast pocket was a beautifully embroidered motif of a standard dress helmet. I must admit I was impressed immediately. His answers to my questions were faultless.

'What kind of gear have you been used to?'

'What have you got, skins or standard dress?'

'We use both, but mainly standard dress.'

'Hard hat is fine with me, or skins with normal air masks.'

'What about underwater burning and welding gear?'

'Again, what have you got, seafire or oxy-arc?'

'We use oxy-arc all the time.'

'Fine,' he said, and it did not dawn on me at that time that he had not answered the welding question. By then I was fairly sure I had myself an experienced diver.

'When can you start?' I asked.

'When do you want me to start?'

'I could do with you starting at eight tonight, on the night shift for a twelve-hour shift. We're pretty desperate for divers at the moment.'

'OK,' he said. 'I'll be here at eight.'

I told him I would stay back to see him started, although by that time I myself would have completed more than a twelve-hour shift.

When I returned to the diving boat, Sandy had completed the panel of piles and the engineers were in the process of dropping down the jigs to the correct level to burn the next five holes in the next eighteen-pile panel. Sandy finished his shift and left the boat on his way home. Dod had only been on duty for four hours, so I asked him if he was willing to go through the night to break in a new diver.

He agreed and I decided to make the new man's first night as simple as possible, by burning the first three holes for him before he arrived. This would leave him with only two holes to burn in a full twelve-hour shift. I was burning away when Dod came on the phone.

'The new gadji is here and getting dressed.'

'OK Dod, when he's ready, tell him to come down my lines.'

Shortly after that I felt a tap on my shoulder and turning around I found the new man beside me. I hit my chin switch and said, 'I'm burning the third of five holes at the moment, so I'm only leaving you two holes to burn through the night. If you want, you can go to my right and have a look at the finished job behind us, that should put you in the picture.'

139

Instead of chinning his switch and speaking to me, he was nodding his head like mad inside the helmet; then he left me. I finished the burning of the third hole, surfaced and headed for home.

When I arrived back the following morning, I met Dod coming up towards the offices, carrying a wet diving suit. After each spell of diving in salt water, a suit requires to be thoroughly washed out with fresh water and dried. This was always carried out in the diving hut on shore. 'Well?' I asked. 'How did it go?'

Dod's face was a picture of absolute disgust. 'Hellish,' he said. 'That guy was never a diver.'

'What happened?' I asked.

'Bobby, that Jerry O'Hara was down at the whaling in South Georgia with us for years. He might have gone swimming sometime in a wetsuit but that would be about all, he was never a diver.'

I could not contain myself. 'Dod, for God's sake, what happened?'

'After you left, he asked for the burning gear and we lowered it down to him, there were all sorts of small explosions under the water and he suddenly appeared on the surface all blown up like the Michelin man. We had a hell of a job getting him right way up and dragging him aboard. We stripped him of the gear and he vomited all over the boat. He couldn't get off the boat fast enough.'

'What time did all this pantomime take place?' I asked.

'He was ashore and running by eleven o'clock, you probably would do better letting Ian and I have a go as trainee divers, we couldn't be any worse than the likes of that gadji,' Dod said.

Dod's last words were turning over in my head as Sandy's brother-in-law, Tam Sutherland, was dressing me aboard the boat. I was impatient to get below to see what damage the cowboy diver had done. I slipped off the ladder and down.

140

'On the bottom Tam,' I said.

'On the bottom it is,' came Tam's response.

When I saw the mess of both the pile and the burning jig I could hardly believe my eyes. The jig fits snugly into the bosom of the pile and is secured by four thumbscrews. It is lowered from the surface to a given level determined by the civil engineer from above. It has a five-inch diameter hole in its centre, the edge of which is insulated so the burning rods don't arc sideways into the jig. The system requires placing the burning rod inside the jig and resting it side-on against the insulation. Now holding the end of the rod about a quarter of an inch away from the face of the pile to be burned, the diver calls for the knife switch to be thrown on. The power flows through the rod and forms an arc across the quarter-inch gap. It also activates a solenoid valve in the torch, which in turn impinges oxygen onto the puddling metal. The Larsson piles are three-quarters of an inch thick and the torch slices through them like they were butter. It takes only minutes for the rod to travel around the inside of the jig and the five-inch diameter hole has been cut through the pile.

I counted sixty-three small holes which had been blown through the pile and fourteen through the jig itself. He must have been stabbing wildly with the torch all over the place but not one of them was inside the five-inch diameter of the jig. Instead they were scattered all over, high and wide, through the uninsulated part of the jig and through the pile high above it.

'Bob, you better come up, there's trouble on the way.' It was Sandy on the phone.

'For God's sake what's happening now?'

'The rowing boat is coming out and Sandy Green is in it.'

I groaned out loud. 'OK! I'm coming up, take up my lines.'

The Dundonian Sandy Green was the SSEB diving inspector, employed directly by the electricity company. He would pay us frequent visits and under the contract we had to provide him with a set of gear and linesmen, when he would dive to inspect our work.

I was on the boat as Sandy Green came aboard. I gave him the story of the cowboy diver's night shift. The Dundonian shook his head saying, 'Silly laddie, he could just as easily have blown a hole through his own helmet, waving the torch about with the knife switch still on.'

'Exactly Sandy,' I said. 'Anyway, you can take a look at the mess he's made and tell me how you want it made good.

Sandy dressed, clambered over the side and was away.

'On the bottom, Bob.'

'On the bottom Sandy,' I repeated on the phone. Shortly after, the swearing began. 'Oh! The bloody fool has made a right mess of this lot.'

'The thing is Sandy, how do we make a silk purse out of that pig's ear of a job?'

'I'm going to take a look at the finished work now,' he said. 'We'll talk aboot the mess when I come up.'

'Fine Sandy, I'm going into the cabin for a sandwich and a coffee, so I'll turn you over to Tam now.'

I stayed in the cabin until Sandy came back on board, stripped off his gear and joined me.

'Sorry Bob,' he said as he came into the cabin. 'I'm afraid you'll have to fill all the holes by welding to get that lot watertight.'

I had been thinking of a solution all the time he had been below, so I said, 'Suppose I get a large plate cut to size to cover the whole lot of the holes, and I put in a run weld all around it, how would that do?'

'Aye, I'd be happy enough with that,' he said. 'And I'll have a look at it the next time I'm aboard. I have to go now, I'm already late for a meeting with my boss.'

That afternoon I was in Eric's office – he had heard about the cowboy and sent for me.

'Sandy Green told me what happened last night,' he said. 'I thought you said you wouldn't start any cowboys on this job.'

'Honestly Eric, he fooled me completely. He spoke and acted like a man who had been at the game for years.'

'Well anyway Bob, we must get more divers. So have you any idea where we might get them from?'

I remembered what Dod had said.

'Eric there's a lot of the work that doesn't need a lot of skill, such as tightening up the nuts of the tie rods with a spanner and wrapping the nuts and the ends of the rods with tape. Also fitting the fishplates to the walings and bolting them together with dozens of small bolts and . . .'

'Get to the point,' said Eric loudly, a man dedicated to brevity and speed.

'OK, suppose I make up some men such as Dod Donaldson and Ian Crow into trainee divers and get them to do all the simple jobs to start with and . . .'

'Do whatever it takes to get this job moving. You're in charge of all the underwater work so *get it moving*.' He calmed down a bit, although he was still a bit wide-eyed as he said in a quieter voice, 'Make up your trainee men but at the same time try to think where we might get more professional divers.'

19

Dodging Death and Boatmen

The morning Buncer started with us as a boatman we climbed aboard the *Tom Eadie*, which had been moored all night in the old harbour at Cockenzie. The tide had turned and began coming in again, but by 8 a.m. she was still resting on the bottom, so there was nothing we could do until she floated. I used the time to explain to Buncer what his duties would be when manning the phone when we were below.

'See that line of lorries,' I said pointing to a convoy queuing up to discharge their loads of red blaize between the finished piles at the east end of the job.

'I see them,' Buncer agreed.

'Well unfortunately they'll keep at it all day today while that bulldozer levels it out to the top of the piles. After it has been levelled and consolidated by the dozer, the surface crew will lay the railway sleepers on it and then the rails and bring the sheer leg derrick forward for the next set of eighteen piles to be pitched and driven.'

'Why did you say unfortunately?'

'Good point Buncer, because the tipping of the red blaize turns the sea blood red and removes all visibility. When I go down this morning, it will be the same as if my helmet had no windows at all. I'll be totally blind and I'll need you to talk me to the job. Now it's simple, when I reach the bottom I'll tell you I'm going to fall forward on my face. As I do this my bubbles will show you which way I'm facing. You can then instruct me to set off left or right or whatever. From then on, watch my bubbles and correct me as I go.'

It was now 8.30 a.m. and the *Eadie* came off the bottom.

'Go ahead Buncer,' I said, 'take her out.'

'Bobby,' he said, 'your uncle used to be a deep-water sailor. I don't fancy this close-shore stuff, at least, not until I know the coastline a bit better. I would rather you took her out for now.'

I saw the sense in his argument, for by that time I knew where every outcrop of rock lay at low water. I took her out and anchored close to the east end of the job, just adjacent to the old harbour we had just left. Dod dressed me and I prepared to dive. I had not yet told Dod and Ian Crow I was intending to take them on as trainee divers. I would have to start linesmen first, to take their place.

I gripped hold of the shot line and pulled. It was fast to the diving ladder. I set off down and reaching the bottom I informed the boat above me. 'On the bottom Buncer. I am now going to fall forward on my face, watch the direction of my bubbles.' I allowed myself to fall forward until I was lying flat on the seabed. I waited for instructions.

'OK,' said Buncer. 'Now stand up and face the job.' What was I hearing? I could not help my reaction as I said, 'Away you barmy bastard, if I knew where the job was I wouldn't need you to talk me to it.'

From then on Buncer became one of the best at talking a blind diver to the precise area he wanted to be in. Over the years to come he would admit how stupid he had felt that day but after that first hiccup he guided me in perfectly and I began fitting fishplates to tie the walings together. All by feel

146

alone, I would push a podger through the bolt holes of the fishplates, then through the waling to line them up, then thread a dozen bolts through both and using two spanners begin to tighten them up. I was working away when Dod came on the phone.

'Bobby!' His voice sounded excited. 'Come back out of there now.'

I was in the process of securing the last two bolts, so I said, 'Can I hold on for five more minutes?'

I was suddenly yanked off my feet and found myself travelling seawards flat out, like a human torpedo. I must have covered about thirty yards when just as quickly as the pull began, my lines fell slack and I was able to regain my feet.

'Right,' I said, 'what happened there, what was that all about?'

There was no reply. If there is one thing that causes concern in a diver's mind, it's being ignored on the diver phone.

'Can I take it you don't want to tell me?'

Again there was no response. There was nothing wrong with my incoming air supply, so I had to consider the possibility that the phone had packed up. I decided to try hand signals, and gripping my lines I sent up an attention pull.

At least I tried to send up an attention pull but instead of feeling the resistance of a linesman's hands, I found I was pulling down more of my own lines. I tried again with the same result. By now I was becoming alarmed.

Had something happened on the boat? If the phone had failed, one of them must surely have signalled to let me know. My main concern was the fact it was obvious nobody was tending my lines. The complete lack of vision was not helping either so I began coiling up my lines as I followed them back. When I reckoned I had sufficient coils in my arms to reach the surface, I dropped them at my feet and gripped hold of the conjoined

147

pipes about six feet from my helmet in my left hand and brought them down to knee level.

Now I was ready to make an unassisted ascent to the surface. By holding the pipes down at my knees, I would not turn upside down if somehow they snagged below me before I reached the surface. Now came the important bit – I must push in my spindle valve and inflate the suit. On the way up I must be careful not to over-inflate or I would finish up on the surface flat out with arms and legs like some bloated monster man. At the same time I must not let too much air escape on the way up, for fear I might lose buoyancy and sink back to the bottom.

I jumped off the bottom and was on my way up. Normally when we spindled up we could look out through our right side light and regulate our speed to equal the ascent of our own air bubbles; I could not do that this time for I would see nothing until my helmet was above the red-coloured sea. I bounced to the surface safely and holding my spindle with one finger I slowly closed the valve under it until my corselet raised slightly above the surface. I was now in full control of my suit. I was also facing the diving boat which was only about twenty-odd feet away. Buncer and Dod were right in the stern of the boat and obviously arguing hotly. Their faces were contorted with rage and their arms were going like windmills. Naturally I couldn't hear what they were saying but I could imagine.

My lines lay forgotten behind the two of them. 'Hey!' I roared loudly. 'You pair of buggers, don't forget the diver!'

There was nothing the matter with the phone for they both jumped at my voice and Dod, seeing me on the surface, made a grab for my lines and began retrieving them from the bottom. It was some time before he had the slack gathered in and began to tow me to the ladder.

They soon got over their fall-out and peace reigned supreme

once more on the *Eadie*. Meanwhile I heard the full story of what had happened between them.

The shore squad had been shifting the last of the A-frames, now they were no longer required, and they had two wire slings made fast to one of them. The derrick swung it slowly to the seaward side and just as it was about to pass over my bubbles one of the slings burst. The frame danced up and down on the one remaining sling directly over the top of my bubbles. When I asked for five minutes more Dod had hesitated and Buncer tore my lines out of Dod's hands and began hauling me hand over hand out from under the frame. This had upset Dod and very nearly started a fight between the two of them. In the heat of the moment they forgot all about me as they raged at each other. I was in the wrong to begin with. I should have dropped everything when Dod told me to come away and of course Dod was wrong by hesitating. Buncer was correct in his action, even though the single sling did not break until the frame was well past the spot I had been working under. The shore squad were also in the wrong by not removing the heavy ballast from the bottom of the frames before slinging them and wrong again for using very light wire slings. Such are the simple little mistakes that human beings make and how they can sometimes add together to bring about real tragedy. Luckily for me all was well that ended well.

20

Shellfish and Herring Galore

I was on the night shift, it was 3 a.m. and I was on the bottom, bolting fishplates tying the walings together. The cluster lamps along the top of the dam were shining down through forty feet of sea water with a brilliance we very seldom experienced. The sea was calm and crystal clear. It was perfect diving weather. Dod was lining me from the boat, anchored about thirty feet away from the dam. Because the nights were beginning to turn colder, I suspected Buncer and Dod would be in the warmth of the cabin above me.

I did not mind, so long as they stayed awake and paid attention to the phone, when I wanted anything. I had a large bag of bolts lying on the sand at my feet, so I had not called up to the boat for almost two hours. Working under these conditions was a real treat, even the tiny fish that crowded around to stare in through my side and front lights did not bother me. Like goldfish in reverse their little eyes goggled in at me with curiosity. They showed no fear, even when I would wave a hand to ward them off, so I could see the next hole, to thread another bolt into place. They merely finned out of reach and as soon as I started to use both spanners again they crowded back, with their little mouths close up to my lights.

I was thinking Eric would get a surprise to find four walings bolted up for a total running length of 108 feet in one night. The reason of course, was due to the perfect vision I had up to then, but sod's law took over and the lights began to dim. Slowly but surely they faded away until total black dark reigned once more.

'What happened to the lights?' I said aloud.

There was no answer. 'Dod, what happened to the lights?' Still no answer. 'Buncer!' I roared.

'Hello. What is it?' Buncer answered in an alarmed tone of voice.

'What happened to the cluster lamps on the dam? I'm in the black dark down here.'

'There's nothing the matter with the lamps up here,' Buncer replied. 'The sea is like glass and it's as bright as day under the lights just now.'

'If the lights are all right, then there must be something really big between them and me and it's shutting out every scrap of light down here. Have a look over the side and see if you can see anything under the surface.'

Dod came on the phone with real excitement in his voice. The words flew out like machine-gun fire.

'Bobby there's a huge shoal of herring stretching in all directions all around us. The boys are loading the boat with pock nets.'

He was off the phone as quickly as he had come on it.

'Dod?' I said. No answer. '*Dod!*' I roared. He came back on with an exasperated tone.

'What is it, Bobby we're trying to net as many as we can before they disappear, can you hang on a minute?'

'No Dod I can't hang on a minute, you're probably netting only small herring on the surface. Tie a sugar sack on my lines and send it down to me. Now listen, as soon as I have the sugar sack I'm going to screw up my exhaust valve and bullet up through the shoal with the mouth of the bag open. You will have to haul me out to the boat, I'll be flat out on the surface out of control but you know the drill. Doing it my way, we'll get a 200-weight sack filled with the larger fish from the mid-water.'

I pulled my lines down to me hand over hand until the sugar sack arrived. Untying it I told Dod to take up all the slack line, opened up the mouth of the sack and holding it open with both hands quickly closed my exhaust valve and again gripped the sack with both hands. I inflated quickly and shot up through the shoal, like a vertical torpedo, and the lads dragged me out to the boat. They took hold of the sugar sack and Dod knew how to correct a diver out of control on the surface. He gripped the back of my helmet by the air intake elbow and lifting slightly used his free hand to unscrew my exhaust valve. The air began to rush out of my suit and my boots slowly began to sink down from the surface. Once more I was in control of my gear. Of course it was impossible to haul the sugar sack aboard until they had nearly half emptied it with the pock nets.

The fish were some of the largest and fattest herring we had seen in a long time.

When the morning light came, our boat looked like a fishing smack. We had some job to try and clean it up and get everything shipshape and Bristol fashion before the day shift arrived to take over. Everyone got a share of the fish including all the squads on the dam head. The herring shoal had been attacked and herded into the face of our dam by grey seals and an enormous shoal of predatory mackerel. At 7 a.m. I came up and, standing on the ladder after Dod had taken off my weights and helmet, I asked for a cigarette before I climbed on board. Sandy lit one and put it between my lips so I could smoke it without touching it with my wet hands. Mr Pascoe, the sub-agent, appeared on the dam head and shouted down to us.

'Bob, before you strip off, can you come round to the inside piles and recover the piling hammer that Old Brass has lost over the side.'

Dod showed how angry he was by saying, 'Why can he not get the day shift to pick it up? We've just finished a twelve-hour shift.' He booted a cork fender out of his way in annoyance.

'Throw the weights and helmet on Dod,' I said, 'and I'll make it a quickie and we can all go home.'

I was unprepared for Dod's reaction, I never saw him move so quickly as he fired on the weights and the helmet, screwed in my front glass, handed me the shot line and slapped the top of my helmet as fast as it takes the time to say it. I slipped off the ladder, before the penny dropped and I realised why Dod was so fast. I still had a lit cigarette gripped in my lips and smoke building up inside my helmet. I knew they would be listening on the phone and grinning while waiting for the coughing and spluttering to begin.

I was determined I would not give them the satisfaction of a laugh at my expense but my God it was hard. I hit the bottom and threw myself face down. I spat out the cigarette onto the inside of the front light and opened my spit cock to suck in a mouthful of sea water and extinguish the cigarette. Now I had to wait as the smoke was blown out of my exhaust valve. My eyes were streaming and my throat was silently protesting its desire to cough out loud but I would not allow it. Recovering somewhat, I carried on with the job I had come down to do and sent the piling hammer back up to Old Brass. I made no mention of Dod's joke at all, as I stripped to go home.

The following night, when I reached the bottom, the conditions were identical to the night before. Every bit as calm and clear, but there was a difference. As far as the eye could see, the bottom was littered with the dead bodies of herring everywhere. Thousands of dead fish covered the sandy bottom, which the night before had shown no sign of living creatures other than an occasional flatfish. Now, feeding on the carnage left behind, were large red-backed edible crabs, with pincers almost the size of my hands, silver eels as thick round their bodies as my forearms, rock codling around two to three pounds in weight, large saithe, fair-sized plaice, golden pollack and even a couple of small turbot. In twelve hours, it seemed, everybody had come to dinner. I told the lads aboard our boat and advised them to get their fishing lines out. I explained to Dod to let some baits lie right on the bottom, where the large crabs would seize them and never let go, and to set other baits about two feet up from the bottom. I then headed in to the job. The night's work was welding up the tie rod plates after the rods had been tightened to the engineer's specification.

This was a job normally done while working blind in murky water, by touch only, with no fear of getting a flash from the welding torch. Tonight I wore a dark glass across my front light and for the first time on that job I could see what I was welding. I came up at midnight for a coffee and a snack and in the cabin I saw a new galvanised bucket boiling away on the cooker.

'What have you got in the bucket lads?'

'Crabs,' Dod answered. 'Big beautiful partan crabs.' He lifted one of the bilge boards. 'Look,' he said. The bilges were alive with them, each one with its nippers tied in the closed position, so they did not injure each other, or destroy the fish lying beside them.

What a catch they had taken aboard in only four hours!

'You lads are going to put the Cockenzie fishermen to shame if you carry on like this,' I said.

'Aye but only if you keep marking our card,' said Dod.

At 1 a.m. I returned to the seabed once more and remembering the lit cigarette in my helmet joke I searched among the dead fish until I found a stinking cod about three pounds in weight. I picked it up. Now I had to find Dod's fishing line. This was not hard to do, for Dod was using green line whereas Billie and Buncer were both working with brown lines. I did not want to make a mistake. The crystal clear water helped and I soon had the rotten fish hanging on Dod's hook. It was with a certain satisfaction I now returned to my night's work.

At seven o' clock that morning I came up to strip off and head back into the old harbour. Dod gave me a strange look as he took off the gear. With a half grin on his face he said, 'I lost about an hour and a half's fishing before I thought there must be something wrong.'

He nodded towards Billie and the Buncer.

'They pair were hauling up fish like there was no tomorrow but you got me that time cousin.'

'I would offer you a cigarette Dod,' I said, 'but I know you've never smoked in your life.'

He smiled, understanding what I meant.

We had to be in the old harbour for 8 a.m.; the day shift would then take over the *Eadie* and return to the dam. We entered the harbour along with two small crab fishing boats with their creels piled up on their decks. As we moored up alongside the quay, one of the crab boats headed towards us, obviously intending to come alongside our boat. One man standing near its bow called to us.

'Would you lads like to buy some freshly caught crabs?' He held up a small crab to show us what they had. Their boat slid alongside us and he got a look into our boat.

'Oh! For God's sake!' he exclaimed loudly. 'Where the hell did you get them?'

Large crabs, at least twice the size of the one he held in his hand, were running all around the bottom boards of our boat.

'Would you consider selling some of them to us?' he asked.

'Sorry,' Dod said quickly. 'We need them all for ourselves.'

'You need all that lot for yourselves?' the fisherman said in amazement.

'We do,' said Buncer. 'We share them with all the gangs on our job.'

Without another word the other fisherman put their boat into reverse and pulled away from us.

'Mind lads,' I said, 'not a word to anyone about where we're getting all the fish and crabs. They will never suspect it's right beside our job. They go well off to set their creels around rocky areas. The dead fish are the only reason these crabs and fish have travelled so far across a flat sandy bottom.'

21

The Fishermen's Revenge

I was standing on the dam head, waiting for Eric Hume to come down to discuss the day's work ahead. It was early morning and Sandy and the rest of the team had gone straight to the old harbour to pick up the *Otter* and bring her out to the job. Today we would be working at the east end of the job, adjacent to the old harbour, which was by now well inshore of our present position. Old Brass was driving a panel of piles ahead of me. He would be using the derrick for about four hours. I had warned him that Eric was coming down to see me. I had to smile as I listened to him talking to his men.

'I don't want any of you to take offence at anything I say to you when the boss is here because I will be shouting at you and calling you all sorts of names but it will be all kidology. You see, if he thinks I'm riding roughshod over you, he will not visit us too often, and that way I can let you all have an easier time of it.'

He turned to the youngest man in the piling gang and dragging out the word *son*, he said, 'Do you understand son?' so loud I felt Eric might hear him from the offices. I had heard it all before, Old Brass had been a ganger man with a squad in the tunnel at Portobello and there he had given his men the same spiel. For instance, when the general foreman, Roddy, would come down the tunnel, Old Brass would start shouting at his men, who were jiggering out the old concrete. 'Come on *lads* I could tear out more concrete with my bare hands, put your shoulders into the jiggers and let's see some action!' He would feign great scorn at their efforts saying, 'Some of you lads would be better suited looking after babies in a nursery. I could get little girls to gun out concrete faster than you can.'

Eric arrived and looking at his watch he said pointedly, 'Where's your diving boat?'

'The harbour is still dry,' I answered. 'They'll be waiting for the *Otter* to float, before they can bring her out.'

'I thought you told me your new boatman, Sam Jarret, was a retired trawler skipper and lived locally.'

'So he is,' I answered. I could see Eric was getting angry.

'Well he must know about the tides, why did he not bring the boat out before it grounded?'

'Because it would have meant taking her out of the harbour three hours ago and you would be paying the crew for a fifteen-hour shift, instead of twelve.'

It was always hard to beat Eric in an argument, and so it proved once again.

'If you don't get the underwater work finished it stops the whole job and I'm paying a damn sight more for all the men on top of the dam doing nothing and losing time on the contract at the same time.'

While we were arguing, Eric was walking closer to the squad driving the piles. I followed him.

'Sandy and I will have all the tie rod holes burned out while Old Brass is using the derrick; after that we won't take long pitching the rods and the night shift will finish all the tightening up. We won't be holding the job back.'

Old Brass had his back to us but the wily old bugger knew

160

we were there. He was looking up at his top man who was attempting to land the Delmag hammer on the top of the next pile to be driven. 'Come oan son!' he roared as if exasperated with his top man. 'If there was hair round it, you would get it in no bother, we don't want they divers blaming us for the job falling behind.'

Eric moved forward to talk to Old Brass and seeing the *Otter* anchoring off the dam, I left them to it.

Sod's law they call it – the incoming tide brought a fairly heavy groundswell with it that day. Heavy enough to affect us on the bottom and I had difficulty holding an arc while attempting to burn the tie rod holes. The tide had to rise almost fifteen feet before we once more had still water on the bottom and I could complete the job. As a result Sandy and I had not finished pitching the tie rods through the holes I had burned. We were four rods short when the night shift arrived. This meant slinging and pitching four half-ton rods, then slinging and placing a twenty-seven foot long waling, weighing three quarters of a ton, just to make up the time lost. Dod and Ian were now diving as trainees on the night shift but they had never, so far, worked with the Henderson derrick and I was reluctant to let them have their first go at it, unsupervised.

'Give us a chance Bobby,' said Dod. 'Ian and I will not let you down, will we Ian?'

'No,' Ian said, 'we will manage it, we won't let you down Bobby.'

'It's not a case of letting me down. It's the fact that your linesmen are pretty inexperienced as well, regarding working with a crane.'

'We'll be fine,' Dod said rather huffily.

So I decided to let them tackle the job, but I would remain there to watch over them for safety's sake.

By eleven o'clock that night everything was going sweetly. I didn't interfere as long as the crew were working to the book. The swell had gone with the ebbing water and the sea was calm once more. We could not have had better conditions, working with a crane – other than the fact we were at the bottom of one of the biggest spring tides of the year. I decided to row myself over to the access ladder up to the dam. I tied the dinghy to it and climbed up. From there it was easier to see how much slew Dod and Ian were putting on the crane, while pitching the rods. Slewing and jibbing were the most dangerous actions when working with a derrick whose jib top was almost two hundred feet above the divers.

All my attention was firmly centred on the job my divers were doing. It took a few minutes for one of the piling men to catch my eye. He was pointing inshore towards the old harbour and shouting something about a fishing boat being in some sort of trouble. Almost at the full extent of the dam's lighting lay the dim shape of a sizable fishing smack. It was very close to the harbour entrance and was just lying there as if moored. Someone on board the smack was shouting to the piling men but no one could make out what they were saying. I looked at the vessel and decided she was in no danger. She sat there on water as still as a mill pond, so I ignored her and turned my attention back to the derrick, which was swinging round with another tie rod to lower down to Dod and Ian on the bottom. From my elevated position I could see my divers' bubbles on the surface. I watched as the linesmen coiled their pipes on the stern of the boat. Both sets of bubbles were heading out away from the dam and towards the *Eadie*. The crane banksman waited until the order came over a power megaphone from the boat to lower away. He signalled the driver to send the rod to the bottom. I watched the crane lower away until the slings fell slack; the rod was on the seabed.

The banksman signalled to the boat and shortly after I could see the twin set of bubbles returning slowly towards the dam. My lads were searching for the rod on the bottom. My young divers were working like true professionals.

One of the piling squad came up to me saying, 'Bob these fishermen are going spare out there.'

'What the hell do they want?'

'We can't make out what they're shouting, but it sounds as if they're pretty angry.'

'Ignore them. I can't afford to be distracted when I have young divers doing a dangerous job.'

The man shrugged and walked back towards his squad. I continued watching the pitching of the tie rods. Once all the rods were in place I watched the crane swinging round with the twenty-seven foot long waling. My divers retreated once more and the piling foreman, Martin Donlevy, alias 'Manhole Heid' came up to me.

'Bob,' he said in his deep, gravelly voice, 'the guys on that boat are going mad with rage at us. Do you want one of my boys to take your dinghy and row out to them and find out what they want?'

By this time I was also feeling exasperated. 'Martin,' I said, 'you know me, if they were in any kind of real trouble, I would be the first to help them. She's a big smack equipped with radio, if her engine has broken down she can call elsewhere for help instead of just lying there at anchor. No, I don't want one of your men to row out to her and I'm not stopping this job for no fishermen.'

'They might be local lads right enough Bob,' Martin laughed, 'trying a bit of revenge on you divers for stealing their fish and crabs.' And off he went, chortling, back to his men.

When the waling was safely down with four tie rods in their

place, the crane was no longer required. I could now go home. I began walking back along the dam head, still carrying my loud-hailer, which I had brought out with me just in case. As I reached Martin's piling squad, I became aware of a faint voice carrying across the water. The fishing smack was still there. I lifted the hailer.

'COME CLOSER THERE IS PLENTY WATER,' I called across. Almost immediately the faint voice increased consider-ably and I heard it.

'There is no water ya BARMY BASTARD.'

I called across to Martin. 'Get one of your men to take our dinghy out to that boat and bring in the man that just called me a barmy bastard.'

I was bristling with rage. Shortly after that, I stood there watching the dinghy returning; it was not coming towards us but heading for the old harbour. As it came nearer I saw two well-dressed men sitting in the stern, one of whom was shaking his fist at me. Close enough now, the man shouted, 'I will see you in the morning.'

It was with the utmost amazement that I recognised Eric Hume.

'Oho!' Martin exclaimed, 'you're for it now Bobby.' He seemed delighted it was my turn to be in trouble. He had been the ganger man in charge of the pump men at Portobello when the dam and tunnel had flooded, the night I fell ill.

In the morning I was waiting in Eric's office for his arrival. I always called him Eric when we were alone but if anyone else was present I always addressed him as Mr Hume. He came in, gave me a hard sideways glance and said, 'You are some man you are.'

'What's the story?' I asked.

Eric hung up his coat then, opening his office door he called, 'Frank? Two cups of coffee.'

He closed the door. 'Do you know who that was with me last night?'

'No, how could I possibly know?'

'That was one of our top directors and we were over in Fife on Mitchells' business. We were delayed so long that he was in danger of missing his flight back to London. We had no chance of making it back by car in time, so he arranged for a driver to bring the Mercedes back today. He then chartered the fishing boat in Kircaldy harbour to take us across the Forth to Cockenzie harbour.'

He stopped the story as the door opened. Frank came in with two cups of coffee and set them on Eric's desk. He left without a word – he was a strange man who always appeared to have a permanent sneer on his face for all workmen and divers.

'We crossed the Forth in no time,' Eric continued. 'Arrived at Cockenzie with loads of time to spare. We found the tide was still ebbing and when the boat skipper tried to enter the harbour he ran onto a sand bar and couldn't get off again.'

'Oh! I thought you were fishermen lying at anchor, waiting for the tide to make enough water to enter the harbour.'

'Well, thanks to you my boss missed his flight. You could have sent a boat out long before you finally did.'

'Eric,' I said indignantly, 'what do you want from me? I had already completed a twelve-hour shift and because the groundswell held us back, I was forced to let my trainee divers use the derrick for the very first time. I had to stay on to make sure they didn't do something stupid, like kill themselves. Also, do you think I would stop the job for some gash fishing boat coming out of the black dark of night and hailing us?'

'Drink your coffee and tell me how I can get some more experienced divers, we have to work from both ends, east and west, at the same time from now on in order to meet the contract deadline.' He was always adept at changing the subject if he felt he might be about to lose an argument.

'I would think your best bet would be to get in touch with a reputable diving company and see if they would hire you some of their most experienced men.'

'What company for instance? Do you have any names for me?'

'You could try Overseas Divers, they're a first-class outfit but make it clear from the start you want men who can weld and burn metal and use explosives under water and also who know how to work with a derrick hundreds of feet above them.'

'Have you got a telephone number for this Overseas Divers?'

'Not off the top of my head but they're an international company Eric, you should have no trouble finding them in the book.'

He rose from behind his desk and lifted the empty coffee cups. 'OK Bob I'll try and contact them and we'll see if a deal can be made.'

He made towards his office door and I opened it for him. It was obvious my spanking was over when he said, 'I won't keep you any longer but I will let you know how I get on.'

22

Overseas Divers

Eric was not able to hire divers directly from Overseas Divers but he decided to give them the east end of the work on a sub-contract basis. He also decided to engage a new general foreman to take over the whole job. He explained he wanted one man to be responsible for all the work and I, as chief diver, would be answerable to this new man. He introduced me to him saying, 'This is Al Matchet, he's a waling and tie rod expert.'

I shook hands with an exceptionally tall man in his early forties. He had an athletic build and red hair and he laughed easily as he said, 'Pleased to meet you Bob, I'm an Irish Canadian, born in Canada of Irish parents, in case you get the idea I've just come over on the boat from Ireland.'

I had the distinct feeling that this was an unhappy man with regard to his Irish heritage. Every Irishman I had ever met in my whole life had been justifiably proud of their Irish ancestry, but not this man.

We got off to a very bad footing straight away because I was unable to hold back from saying, 'What the hell is a waling and tie rod expert, I've never heard of such a thing.'

This did not exactly endear him to me from the word go and we were at crossed swords from that moment onwards. Before he arrived Eric had made the point that he wanted me to remain permanently working on the west side of the job and allow the Overseas Divers to run their own sub-contract on the east side. This meant Sandy and I, with our linesmen, Tam Sutherland and Billie Manclark, and boatman Buncer had all been aboard the *Eadie* until my trainees began working with the derrick. Thereafter we were to alternate week and week about on day shift and night shift with the crew on board the *Otter*, so I had Sandy and Dod swap over boats. I felt happier knowing the *Otter* had Sandy on board looking after young Ian Crow. Shortly after the switchover I was at home, sleeping prior to going on night shift, when Sandy arrived.

'What are you doing here at this time?' I asked. 'Nothing wrong I hope.'

'We never got the tie rods tightened up, so we pulled out early.'

'Why not?' I asked. 'Don't tell me there's another heavy sea running.'

'No, the weather's fine. Do you know what the expert did?'

'No, what did our blown-away Irishman do now?'

'He got our shore squad to smear the threads of the rods with motor grease. I tried to get them to clean it off but it didn't work and they spent what was left of the day burning it off.'

'Why did you not get the shore lads to grab some of the top squads' rods just to let you finish the shift and let me argue with our expert later?'

'Because he got the top squads to grease every rod on the fucking job,' Sandy said angrily. His face was suffused with a blood-pressure red. 'The fucking idiot has done them all, the top rods, the mid-water rods and the bottom rods.' He looked ready to blow a gasket.

'OK! Leave it with me, I'll go see Eric first thing in the morning.'

'Bobby, for God's sake get that Irish clown off our backs,' Sandy said, shaking his head sadly as he left.

Early next morning I was in Eric's office.

'You have to tell him to leave us and our shore squad and our gear alone, we can't work this way.'

'He was trying to help Bobby, anybody can make a mistake.'

'This is not like you Eric, we've lost time on a full panel because our so-called expert didn't know that grease underwater reacts like a thick glue and it becomes impossible to run a nut onto the thread of the rod, even by hand, never mind trying to tighten them up with a spanner.'

'I'll have a word with him, but I have a more serious matter I want to discuss with you.'

I must admit at that time, I thought this was Eric's usual ploy at changing the subject but no, this time it was genuine.

'The Overseas Divers have hit a snag and their end has been stopped for two days, so now they're holding the whole job back.'

'You said you wanted me to leave their end alone and . . .'

'I *now* want you to get that problem solved and get that end moving again.'

This was the old dominant Eric speaking once more. 'It has something to do with a jammed waling that they can't get either on or off. Go over there Bobby and find out what's wrong and for God's sake *fix it*.'

When I climbed on board the *Eadie* Dod had not started suiting up.

'Matchet said I was not to get dressed, he said something about us going over to the harbour side this morning.'

'Yes I know Dod, I've just come from Eric's office, he wants us to help the Overseas squad out.'

Buncer came out of the cabin. 'What does he want us to fly at this morning?' he asked.

'I don't know Buncer, we have to weigh anchor and get ourselves over the other side and find out what has stopped them dead over there.'

Matchet appeared on the dam above us and shouted, 'Bob, get over to the east side and get that problem sorted out.'

Now no man can change his nature; I could not stop myself from shouting back.

'Al, both you and the boss want to make up your fucking minds, one minute it's don't go near the other side, leave them with their own sub-contract. The next minute it's get yourselves over there; and another thing Al, what were you doing greasing rods that were going to be used underwater?'

He ignored me and marched away with a disdainful down-sweep of one hand. Oh! How I was beginning to hate that man.

'What do you mean he greased the rods?' my linesman Billie Manclark asked as we sailed to the other side. Billie was an out of work shipwright friend of Sandy I had taken on as a linesman to give him a job.

'The stupid bastard greased the threads of every rod on the job,' I answered.

'Oh my God,' said Billie, 'the underwater rods, what a daft thing to do. You won't get them to work with grease on them.'

'I *know* that Billie, but our Irish expert knows better than we do,' I said dryly.

When we pulled alongside the Overseas boat, which was a small fishing smack, there were two young men sitting either side of the wheelhouse. They were both suited up and wearing full boots and corselets. One had jet-black hair and the other was as fair as the first man was dark. I asked, 'What's the trouble lads?'

'We have a waling stuck,' the fair-haired lad said, with his lower lip sulking.

'We can't get it on and we can't get it off,' said the dark-haired boy sadly.

'Where's Jack Sayers or Tony Sparrow?' I asked.

'Both on holiday,' they answered together.

'And where's Big Geoff?'

They looked blankly at each other.

'I think he was taken away to do another job,' said the blond boy.

In more ways than one, the two youngsters appeared to be right out of their depth, so I said gently, 'OK boys, I'll go down and have a look.'

I got dressed and slid down the shot line.

'On the bottom,' I said.

'You are on the bottom,' came Buncer's repeat.

'Pretty good vision,' I said, 'but then I wouldn't expect anything else since no lorries have been tipping for two days.'

'Tickety-boo,' Buncer acknowledged.

I moved forward. 'Bear left,' said Buncer.

'Bearing left it is.'

A short distance on and Buncer came through again.

'That's it, now straighten up and steady as you go.'

'Straighten and steady it is,' I repeated. Buncer had come on a long way, for now I could see the black wall of the piles emerging slowly from the greeny-blue haze of the sea.

'You're there,' said Buncer.

'I am indeed,' I replied.

I could not believe what I was looking at. In front of me was the mangled remains of a waling. Its top surface resembled a switchback holiday park ride. Along its full length it undulated up and down violently and the rods coming through it were cranked upwards and permanently bent.

'My God!' I exclaimed involuntarily.

'What's up?' said Buncer.

'I'll tell you shortly, after I've had a good look all round.'

I leaned over the top of the twisted remains and found its back face was at least six inches away from the sheet piles – it was indeed neither on nor off its place.

'I'm looking at a real butchered job down here Buncer.'

'Really bad eh?' It was Dod on the phone. 'Do you want the derrick round, I can see Murphy from here.'

'No, Dod, it'll be a while before I can use the derrick on this mess but you could give Murphy a shout and tell him to come aboard. I'll come up to talk to him.'

Back on the diving ladder, I could see Murphy sipping a mug of coffee. I also noticed the two young lads still sitting there in the same position as before. Somehow they reminded me of the two huge statues of a seated Rameses in Egypt. Not a muscle moved and they both stared straight ahead through what appeared to be unseeing eyes.

As soon as Billie had removed my helmet Murphy said, 'The lads are telling me you have a bit of a job on your hands Bob.'

'Do you know anything about it Shaun?' I asked the Irishman.

'I do, to be sure, to be sure, for was I not the man driving the beast that night?' he laughed loudly, nodding towards the two young divers on their boat about fifty yards away. 'Sure it was these two monkeys there that did it.'

'Tell me about it?' I asked. 'Because they never did that lot with ordinary twin slings.'

'Not at all, not at all, sure they broke them both in the first hour and they had one of the welded lifting eyes off, in no time at all. After that they asked for heavier wire strops, to use them singly, so we gave them five-inch wire strops. They could not break them, although the ones they used will never lift anything again.'

Murphy was enjoying himself but I was horrified at what I was hearing.

172

'What sort of weight were the strops taking?' I asked.

'Oh! Around three or four tons to begin with,' he answered gleefully.

'What the hell do you mean to begin with? Don't tell me they asked for more than four tons to lift a three-quarter ton waling.'

'No, to be sure they did not, but with a four-ton strain on, they told me to jib up and I did so, but I stopped when I reached a seven-ton pull.'

I caught my breath. 'Seven tons,' I gasped, 'Shaun, you could have killed them.'

'No Bob, they could have killed themselves. I just obeyed their orders.'

'Shaun, the golden rule has always been give the diver everything he wants except death. You knew better than these two bairns what was going on, did you not tell them?'

Murphy was becoming really annoyed. 'I did, to be sure, time and time again, I called out the purchase weight and my banksman gave them the jib angle. They ignored it all and kept calling for more pull.'

'You should have refused to carry on before something gave way.' I thought Murphy was going to have a fit.

'I did refuse, why do you think the job was stopped? I told the general foreman I would not be held responsible if somebody got hurt and he stopped the job and brought these two monkeys up. That was two days ago.' By this time Murphy was shouting.

'My apologies Shaun, you did the right thing. I have the full picture now. Obviously these youngsters have never had any experience of working with a derrick.'

I called our shore squad and told them to set up our burning and welding generator on the dam head. I also despatched a messenger to the offices to let Eric know I would require another six boxes of burning rods and two boxes of welding rods to be brought on site, over and above what I already had in the divers' store. While we were preparing for the work, Sandy Green, the diving inspector, arrived and decided he wanted to have a look at the damage. The lads got him dressed and down he went. While he was below Matchet arrived and called down to the boat.

'When are you going to make a start Bob?'

I pointed down to the bubbles, which he obviously hadn't noticed. 'Soon as the inspector agrees with what I intend to do, to put it right.'

'Oh! Right,' he said, and off he went. If rushing about a job could possibly speed it up, then our expert would have finished the whole contract long before now.

Sandy Green came up and the boys stripped him of the suit.

'Man I have never seen anything like that before.'

'Pretty bad Sandy eh? I reckon it'll take some time to get that sorted out.'

'How are you planning on tackling it Bob?'

'I'm going to cut across the centre of each low point in turn.'

'The metal will just slam shut again with the strain that's on it.'

'I realise that Sandy, but the rod will blow away about three-eighths of an inch of the metal each time I cut across the width of the waling.'

'Ah! I see where you're going Bob but that will take an awful lot of burning rods and a hell of a long time before you get any piece clear for lifting away. Have you considered you'll be into saturation diving long before the job is done?'

'Yes I realise that Sandy, but once I'm saturated I may as well complete the job and get the tie rods clear before starting to decompress myself, rather than bring another man into saturation with me.'

It took some time to set everything up and because of that it was four o'clock in the afternoon before I started the dive.

I was in fifty feet of water and the mangled waling was about two feet above the sand. In order to cut through the bottom part of the waling I was obliged to kneel on the seabed. I knelt down and gripped the waling with my left hand, clear of my intended cut. I held the torch in my right hand and said, 'Knife switch on.'

Buncer repeated immediately, 'Knife switch on Bobby.'

Now I waited, while my order was called up to the dam and obeyed. I felt the pulse of six hundred amps flow through the torch before Buncer reported, 'The knife switch is on.'

The fact that the waling was six inches away from the face of the piles helped greatly and I was able to cut cleanly across the full seventeen inches of the bottom member without fear of blowing holes through the piles. I was not prepared for the shock generated by the metal slamming closed again at the very end of the cut. I moved along and began the second cut, keeping my helmet and body clear of the metal as it leapt upwards with a crash. This time I was prepared for the shock.

I had to travel along the full twenty-seven feet, making five individual cuts, before the bottom member had straightened the tiniest little bit. The top member was exactly the same. Now I had to cut along the same lines I had completed earlier and again both sides slammed shut once more and with only slightly less force than the first cut. This was going to be a long, long job. The brass ends of the burnt-out rods were building up in my apron – we saved them up, rather than throw them away, every time we fitted a new rod into the torch.

It was a bit of a surprise to me to hear Sandy McGill's voice come over the phone. 'How's it going mate, do you want me to get dressed?'

175

'Well hello Sandy, what are you doing here at this time?'

'What do you mean, at this time? It's half past eight at night and you do remember I'm on the night shift, don't you?'

'Really Sandy, is that the time? I can hardly credit that. No, don't bother getting dressed, I'm into saturation now so I'll carry on. You may as well be comfortable in the meantime.'

'OK Bob, just give me a shout when you've had enough.'

I carried on working my way along the full length of the waling and back again. It was slowly straightening out into six separate pieces. I was cutting away at one of the centre pieces when I got the fright of my life. It suddenly leapt upwards with a loud bang and a screech that almost deafened me.

'Are you all right? Buncer asked anxiously.

With my heart going like a trip hammer I answered in what I hoped sounded like a calm, assured way. 'No problem,' I said quietly. 'What you heard there was the waling tearing itself into two halves. I'm winning.'

Buncer came back instantly. 'I should hope so,' he said, 'it's after midnight, got any idea how long it will take you from now on?'

'No idea at all Buncer, I've never tackled anything like this in all my life.'

The hours now seemed to fly by, after the encouraging splitting in two of the waling. I was on my guard when the next piece slammed downwards and screamed as if in agony,

'OK mate?' It was Sandy this time.

'Fine Sandy, I now have it in three separate pieces but I won't be able to clear anything until it's cut into six parts.'

Slowly but surely the tortured metal was beginning to relax and I called for the derrick to be readied. At last a cut remained open after I finished it. From that moment the work became simple: I would cut one piece clear and send it up on the derrick;

I would have the next ready to go by the time the derrick came back down to me. At five o'clock in the morning I started my decompression time, ascending ten feet at each stop. My last stop was at ten feet under the boat and there I had to remain for seventy-five minutes. I could plainly see the foot of the diving ladder above me. I never was so pleased to hear Buncer say, 'OK Bobby, that's it, you can come up now.'

As I clambered up the ladder, I looked out of my left light and into view came the Overseas Divers' little fishing smack. Either side of its wheelhouse, in the same order I had first seen them, sat my two Rameses lookalike figures, full suit, boots and corselets. As soon as Billie took my helmet off I asked, 'What time is it?'

Billie looked at his watch. 'Twenty past ten, you've been underwater for more than eighteen hours.'

I inclined my head towards the two young divers. 'They were sat like that when we came over here at two o'clock yesterday afternoon.'

Sandy came out the cabin saying, 'They climbed on board their boat at eight o'clock this morning, got dressed and sat just as you see them now.'

'Oh that's not so bad, I thought for a minute they had sat there like that since yesterday afternoon.'

And so ended one of the longest and most awkward jobs I ever did under water.

23

Shipwrecked

Sandy and I were both working away independently of each other. He was tightening up tie rods and I was welding the sealing plates that made the seaward side of the piles watertight. For some strange reason Sandy could not stand the hiss of my air in his helmet, when I would hit my chin switch to speak to him. Without fail, and within seconds of me passing a message, Sandy would always chin his switch to throw the noise of his air back into my helmet. He would not say anything, and to be honest I never worried about the hissing of his incoming air, or for that matter the sound of him grunting with the effort of tightening up the rods.

In the past we once had a duel with our chin switches, which took place without either of us saying a word. He hit his switch and as soon as I realised he did not intend to speak to me, I hit mine. I thought it was all being taken as a bit of sport, so as soon as he hit his again, I did likewise. It became a bit frantic, as we sent the switch back and forth rapidly, and still believing it was only a bit of fun. I chinned it and held it there with my chin. I smiled to myself, for now Sandy was unable to throw it back as long as my chin held it over. Within minutes I got a call from the boat.

'Bob you're driving Sandy mad, he's cursing and swearing

something awful. He says he can't concentrate on what he's doing with the noise of your air distracting him.'

From that day onwards, to the present time, I allowed my mate to have his own way.

I could still hear him grunting and then finally complaining, 'I've had enough of this, take up my lines, I'm coming up for a break and a smoke.'

I carried on with my job of welding the plates and shortly Sandy came on the phone.

'Bobby you'd better come up, the weather's getting up and it looks like we're in for a bit of a blow.'

'OK Sandy. Turn the knife switch off and take up the welding torch.'

My gear was soon cleared from the bottom and I prepared to surface.

'Take me away,' I called as I left the bottom.

On the surface, a bit of a shock awaited me. A fair old sea was running and the boat was rising and falling a considerable distance. One minute it was way above me and the next it was well below me. It becomes a tricky business trying to gauge your move onto the ladder. I had to judge it just right, as I would be falling into the trough of one wave, while the boat was coming up on another. I had to leap on the bottom rung and hang on for dear life before climbing on board.

While Sandy and I were stripping off, we asked the boys on the dam to get the shipping forecast. The answer came back: Force 8, possibly Force 9, with the full tide. At that time we were at half ebb so we had some time in hand. We weighed anchor and set off for the old harbour. Arriving at the east end of the job, where we could see the harbour entrance, we could see we would not be going in there. Some fairly high rollers were running through the mouth of the harbour. Our boatman, Sam

Jarret, suggested laying off shore to a deep-water buoy that the trawlers used when they could not make the harbour. This was sound advice and yet Sandy said, 'How far off is this buoy?'

'Sandy, if you can't make it to a port in a storm and you have a seaworthy boat, get off the shore.'

Old Sam Jarret agreed with me and said, 'It's not far out Sandy, but far enough to ride out a storm.'

We were not long in reaching the buoy and mooring to it.

Time went by and the *Eadie* rose and fell with no problem at all, other than the crew giving way to sea sickness. Only old Sam and myself were unaffected. Some six hours later, I was starving and asked if any of the crew had any food left in their lockers. Tam Sutherland volunteered some pork chops he had. They were the type of chops that had a kidney in their centre and an outer layer of pure fat. I started frying them up on our cooker. Sandy was disgusted, saying, 'For God's sake Bobby, are we not suffering enough without you frying greasy pork chops.'

The wind increased in strength and the *Eadie* began seriously jerking against her mooring wires, which were very light. I went to the bow and watched for a while but all appeared to be bearing up fine. I returned to the warmth and the comfort of the cabin. Each bunk held a groaning, sick man, head lolling over the side, still trying to throw up into a bucket below him. By now there was nothing left in their stomachs to throw up. Old Sam moved from one to another of them in a continual round, trying to help by holding each man's head whenever the retching and straining began. I emptied the buckets over the side and washed them out again. I felt thankful that sea sickness was something that I had never been troubled with.

That night appeared to be particularly long and in the small hours of the morning the wind picked up a far greater momentum. Sam and I had to wedge ourselves in, either side of the air reservoir tanks, to avoid being thrown all over the inside of the cabin. The angry sea hurled itself against us with an even greater fury than before. We were now shipping water over the bows with every wave but that did not worry us. The *Eadie* was designed to take water over her bows and shed it overboard again, before it reached the diving cockpit. What did worry me was the fact I could no longer reach her bows and see for myself what was happening up there. It was obvious the tugging on her mooring post up forward was steadily increasing in violence. Two hours later I knew something had to give: either the light wires would break, or they would rip the mooring post out of the boat. I fervently hoped it would not be the latter, for if that happened, the boat could not survive.

It was with a sense of relief I heard the 'twang' of the first wire severing. Sam immediately vanished into the engine room compartment and started up the engine. The second wire also gave up the ghost and we were adrift. Our crew leapt out of their bunks with an alacrity that sick men were not supposed to have. I took the wheel and presented her port shoulder to the waves, for Sam had given me half speed ahead. The *Eadie* rode the waves easily and was in no immediate danger as long as she remained with her shoulder onto the weather. Sandy came up behind me saying, 'You're not going to take her further out are you?'

'No, I'm just maintaining steerage way on her at the moment, while we think this out.'

'I don't want to be too far out, if we have to swim for it. It's all right for the rest of you, because you're all good swimmers, but I'm not.'

'I don't think it will come to that Sandy, we have plenty of fuel on board, enough to ride the storm out.'

Tam Sutherland had joined us and heard the conversation. 'I

wouldn't like to try swimming ashore on a rocky coast like that,'
he said. 'Is the boat all right so far Bobby?'

'She's fine Tam, so long as we keep her shoulder on to the
sea,' I answered.

'But that's taking us further out all the time,' Sandy argued
and as if in answer to his prayers the engine began spluttering
and died.

The *Eadie* fell off the wind and very quickly turned side-on
to the weather. She began shipping water at the stern. We got
the hand bilge pump working and the lads started baling out
with buckets. I gave Sam a hand trying to find out what had
stopped the engine. We were now drifting towards the shore and
the rocks. Sam and I had checked out the fuel pump and carbu-
rettor and everything appeared normal. We tried the starter motor
again and this time the engine fired up – she was running, but
not sweetly, so I told Sam to operate the throttle by hand and
rushed back up to the wheel. We were within a quarter of a mile
of the shore. I brought her back up into the wind, and once
more set her port shoulder to the waves. Slowly we began pulling
away from the shore.

'You're not going away out to the buoy again are you?' Sandy
said, and his face was a mixture of anger and anxiety.

'Believe me Sandy, I just want to keep her clear of the rocks.
We dare not try and grab hold of the buoy in this wind anyway,
we might smash into it and hole the *Eadie*.'

While we were talking the sound of the engine began faltering
and fading, followed by a burst of power as Sam gave it more
throttle.

'Here, Sandy, take the wheel and keep her on the same heading,
I want to nip down and give Sam a hand. Whatever happens we
won't survive without an engine.'

Between us, Sam and I kept the engine running with its up

and down of revolutions. We were concentrating hard on making sure it did not die on us again and were quite unprepared when we suddenly found ourselves engulfed by water. We were soaked to the skin before it drained down into the bilges.

I called out loudly to Sandy, 'Keep her head up into the wind!' I was thinking he had allowed her to fall off, side-on. I could not know at that time that Sandy had turned the *Eadie* around and was heading back for the shore. We strove manfully to keep that engine running. I then became aware that our stern was lifting first with every wave and realisation came to me with a rush. We were running *before* the waves. I dashed up top and no more than two hundred yards in front of us lay the old harbour mouth. The tide was at half ebb and I could see the white-topped waves breaking over the sand bar outside the harbour – the same sand bar that had prevented the big boss man from catching his plane.

'Oh Sandy!' I groaned, 'you've finished us for sure.'

There was no room left to turn the boat and there was no chance we could possibly clear the sand bar. The only thing in our favour was the fact that the rocks were on either side of the harbour and we were about to founder on pure sand. With a bone-jarring crash the *Eadie* smashed into the sand bar. For a few seconds the bow was buried in the sand and the next wave swung the boat side-on and floated her high above the bottom. She came down harder the second time and swamped. We were all washed overboard, after she sank.

We swam for the harbour mouth and the waves drove us through at speed. We were swept on relentlessly towards the shore and the power of the waves tossed us up on the beach like some little pieces of driftwood. The backwards undertow sucked us back beneath the next breaker, which in turn heaved us ashore again. At last we all managed to escape the waves' cruel game and crawl up the beach to the grass, where we collapsed exhausted.

Waiting there for us was Eric and with him stood Al Matchet.

'Are you all right lads?' Eric asked.

Sandy looked at the rest of us. 'I think so, other than the skin the sand tore off us coming ashore.' He rubbed the abrasions on his arms.

'Don't worry about your boat boys,' said Matchet. 'We'll salvage her after the storm goes and I'll have her back in service in a fortnight.'

I thought, don't talk rubbish man, but I said, 'If she was in deeper water, you might have a chance Al, but at the moment she'll be taking one hell of a beating from these waves.'

'Bob, believe me I'll have her back for you in a fortnight.'

I was too exhausted to argue with him.

Two days later, the sea was as calm as it could be and we were over the top of the *Eadie* in the *Otter*. We could see her clearly, lying on the seabed. Sandy and I made a preliminary dive to assess her overall condition. She had sunk down into the sand bar until her gunnels were flush with the seabed.

'We'll need to use air lifts to clear the sand away from her hull,' Sandy said.

'Yes,' I agreed. 'Look at this Sandy.'

Up forward there were splits across her gunnel on both the port and starboard side. 'That's been caused by the mooring wires before they broke.'

Sandy came round to the bow and had a look. 'Oh! That's the wires right enough,' he agreed, 'but to be honest Bob, I thought she would be in a far worse condition than she is.'

'So did I Sandy, so did I.'

We had arranged for the derrick to be brought back on its rails until it was opposite our position. From there, with its jib almost horizontal, it could reach over the *Eadie*'s position. We also had a four-inch Lister pump brought out to us on a raft. On our second dive, Sandy didn't take long to blow away all the sand from around the boat using a six-inch air lift. Meanwhile I placed the lifting wires under her, while the spreader bars stayed above her cabin top. We had to be careful with the lift for she was a heavy boat and she had more than a ton of ballast on board. When all was ready, I had the derrick take the strain and no more. I surfaced and had my helmet removed. I called up to the banksman. 'Tell the driver to bring her up slowly and stop when her gunnels are just above the surface and no more.'

This would be a bit of trial and error as we didn't know whether she was holed below the waterline or not. The derrick driver brought her up ever so slowly, and stopped with her gunnels only inches above the surface. Our boat towed the raft alongside and set the Lister pump's intake pipe inside the *Eadie*. With its delivery pipe in the sea, the lads started the Lister and the water poured out of the boat. To the relief of all of us, she came up high and handsome and proved her hull was sound. Her sides were sore scarified all over by the abrasive action of the sand being driven against her with a far greater force than any sand-blasting machine.

When we came ashore, after towing the *Eadie* into the old harbour, we were met by Al Matchet who said, 'Right lads, I'll have her operational again within a fortnight.'

'Al,' I said, 'you have no chance of getting that boat back in the water, completely repaired, in a fortnight.'

I do know he had Weatherheads boatyard working round the clock on it, but damn me if he didn't manage it and prove me wrong.

24

The Birler

The *Eadie* was returned to us in mint condition. Al Matchet had worked a small miracle as regards putting her back in service within a fortnight and especially with a brand-new look. She had been completely re-sprayed with fibreglass which shone with the gleam of a new shilling. It was unfortunate that his next venture, which was a truly inspired idea, should finish up so tragically. He really deserved a better result.

Up to that time, all our piles were shipped to Leith docks in seventy-five foot lengths. We had a team of men permanently working in the port. Their job was to cut the base of each pile into a 'vee' shape and fit rock shoes, so they could be driven down through the layers of sandstone. They were then transported by heavy haulage contractors to our site and stacked, by crane, in a storage yard near the offices.

This meant they were double handled by mobile cranes before they could be brought within reach of the Henderson derricks, which were progressing steadily out to sea. Al thought up the brilliant idea of having Henry Robb's shipyard make a fifty-foot long, heavy duty raft capable of floating eighteen piles at a time and towing them from Leith straight to within reach of the derricks. Weather permitting, this was a vast improvement on the old method, as eighteen piles made up one panel, so every two trips completed a section.

Birler Smith, another old trawlerman, was entrusted with the job of ferrying the raft back and forth to Leith by towing it with the *Otter*. He was given two men to assist him. All the Port Seton men called John Smith the 'Birler' and I had to ask how he came by his nickname. I was told it came from his father, who was also John Smith and had died as a middle-aged man, whereas his mother survived him to a ripe old age. When she eventually died and went to heaven, she found Saint Peter on the Gate. In reply to her enquiring about her husband, Saint Peter said, 'Madam we have countless thousands of John Smiths up here, can you give me any clues which might identify your husband?'

'Yes, all our married life I would ask him, at different times, if he had ever been unfaithful to me. He always replied, "If I have ever been unfaithful to you my dear, may I turn in my grave".'

Saint Peter laughed and said, 'Oh! You mean Birler Smith.'

One late October night, Sandy and I had finished our shift and we were stripping out of our gear and preparing to take the *Eadie* back to the old harbour. It was 7.10 p.m. and quite dark. We heard Al Matchet's voice hailing us from the dam, just as we were hauling up the anchor. 'Bob, the *Otter* left Leith three hours ago and she's not turned up, can you take your boat up the Forth and look for her?' I turned our spot headlight up on the dam and there stood Matchet, shielding his eyes against the glare of the spot.

'Is she towing a raft of piles?' I asked.

'Yes, and she should have been here long ago, can you go and find her?'

'OK Al, we'll head out now,' I called back up to him.

The sea was calm and the spot lamp showed the way ahead

for a considerable distance, so at first we were travelling quite fast. Very soon we encountered the first signs of sea fog and as we moved up the Forth so the fog thickened. I asked Buncer to cut her speed as the lamp was now bouncing back off the fog and we had greatly reduced vision up forward. Sandy tried shouting with the powered megaphone and we would listen intently, but there was no answer and the only sound was the 'thrum' of our own engine and the soft 'swish' of our propeller. We cut speed once more to slow ahead and by now we were steering by compass only.

'I don't like this,' I said to Sandy as we both peered ahead of the boat. 'That bloody raft is only fifty feet long and the piles overhang it forward and aft.'

'I think we should shut the engine down and I'll try the megaphone again,' Sandy said.

'Shut her down Buncer, and we'll listen again after Sandy has another go with the megaphone.'

'HELLO!' Sandy roared out over the placid water and we all listened again. This time we picked up the very faintest sound of a voice. It appeared to come from the seaward side of us.

'Start her up Buncer and head nor-nor-east,' I said. We carried on, still at slow ahead, and every so often we stopped to listen. The voice floating back to us was gaining in strength, so we were going in the right direction. I was now worried on two counts – firstly the fear of running into the piles and secondly we were now approaching the main shipping lane for Leith and Granton. I said nothing to worry the lads but I knew we could be run down by a merchant ship at any time. The fog was clearing slowly the further off the shore we travelled, but any merchant ship would not be expecting a small vessel in her path.

Into the beam of our headlight came a strange sight. Two men were standing on top of the piles and waving to us. The Birler sat on the piles with his head buried in his hands. There was no sign of the *Otter* anywhere. All three of them were frozen to the marrow as they had been drifting out to sea for hours with the cold clammy fog eating into their bones like some predatory animal.

In the cabin of the *Eadie* they soon thawed out, sitting around the heater and drinking steaming hot mugs of freshly brewed coffee. By the time we made the raft fast and got her in tow the fog had gone and we could see we were fairly close to Inchkeith island. The sky above us filled rapidly with stars and a crescent moon appeared and helped drive away some of the darkness of the night. In the distance, around seven or eight miles away, were the lights of Leith docks.

Sandy saw them and said, 'I think we should head for Leith; we can moor the raft and the *Eadie* alongside the outer harbour. She'll be safe there for the night.'

'That's what we'll do Sandy,' I agreed. 'We can phone the job from there and let them know everything is fine and in the morning we'll tow the raft back to Cockenzie.'

We set off up the Forth towards Leith, and the Birler sat in the cabin with his hands covering his face and his head down on his knees. I caught the eye of one of the young men beside him and motioned with my head that I wanted him to join me in the stern of the boat. He came out of the cabin so I could speak to him privately.

'What happened and where's the *Otter*?' I asked him.

'Well,' he answered, 'we left Leith and only got to the far end of Portobello beach when the raft started crabbing sideways. The Birler told us he was going to come astern and we were to take up the slack of the tow rope. He then went full ahead to try and tug the raft around and it worked, but we were now pulling the raft at some speed and he tried to turn the *Otter* out of the way

190

but he couldn't manage it. The raft was swinging around wildly and three of the piles smashed through the side of the *Otter*. She sank very quickly and the three of us had to jump on the raft before she went down.'

'Can I take it you were towing the raft with the rock shoes of the piles facing you?' I said.

'Yes, that's right. The towing bollards are at either end of the raft but it depends on how the shore lads load them on.'

'Well, it's easy to be wise after the event but I don't think I'd be very happy looking at eighteen potential torpedoes menacing my boat.'

We arrived at the long run into Leith docks, which were still tidal at that time, and having obtained the harbour master's permission to bring the raft in through the fairway we sailed right up, close to the Prince of Wales dry dock, and made fast behind the Commission's own diving boat.

In the morning Sandy introduced me to the Commission's divers. Martin Bendicks, who had been the only diver the port employed for almost ten years on a full-time basis, until the law changed in 1957 requiring divers to work in pairs, and Tom 'Spud' Murphy, the man who took over Jimmy Ward's job after Jimmy was killed at Kircaldy harbour.

We had an uneventful run down the coast in the morning, on a calm sea shimmering in the sunshine emanating from a clear sky devoid of clouds, and the only sad thing about the whole affair was the Birler could not live down his title of the man who torpedoed himself.

25

The Red Mist

Early one Thursday morning I called into the offices before starting work. I wanted to see Frank, our timekeeper, to arrange a sub, or in other words, a draw on the lying time wages so I could pay off a rather large bill. Frank had his usual perennial sour face in place and it steadily built into a look of pure hatred as he said sarcastically, 'A one hundred pounds a week diver, asking for a twenty pound sub, I don't think so.'

'Look Frank, I don't care if you take the full twenty pounds off again the following week, just so long as I have the money tomorrow night, OK?'

'That will be right,' Frank answered. 'A tradesman earns eighteen pounds a week and asks for a sub of around five at the most, and you want twenty.'

'That's right Frank,' I said, 'I will call in at finishing time tomorrow to collect it.'

As I left the time office Frank called out again, 'Huh! I don't think so.'

At seven o'clock that night, I was on the bottom underneath the *Eadie*, waiting for a waling to be landed on the seabed so I could locate it and manoeuvre it into its place. For the first time ever I felt the thump of its arrival on the bottom. 'The waling is down,' Buncer informed me.

'Tickety-boo,' I replied, and set off searching the sea bed ahead of me to find it. It was almost buried in the sandy bottom and I realised it must have been dropped with some force. I was instantly on my guard and made sure my lines were behind me as I placed the palms of my hands on its front face.

'OK! Just grip it,' I said.

'Grip it, it is,' said Buncer.

The next minute the waling shot up almost five feet and began bouncing violently up and down.

'Hold it!' I called with alarm, as I barely managed to keep my palms on its face.

'Hold it, it is,' Buncer replied, followed by, 'All held Bobby.'

'Buncer, bring it down about two feet, carefully.' Buncer repeated my order once more and I waited some time before the waling suddenly slammed into the bottom with a far greater force than before. I immediately abandoned the job, saying, 'Take up my lines, I'm coming up.'

Back on board the boat, I quickly had the lads undress me completely, jumped aboard the dinghy, rowed over to the dam and climbed up. I gathered our shore squad together and approached the derrick, which was in darkness.

'Hello?' I called up to its cabin. 'Who's driving tonight?'

The door of the cabin opened and Shaun Murphy stood there swaying, as he held onto the door of the cabin with both hands.

'Well hello there Bob, sure it's meself that's driving the beast tonight.'

With one hand he reached into his back pocket and pulled out a half bottle of whisky.

'Come on up Bob and we'll have a drink together.'

'No Shaun, you come down and we will have one down here,' I said.

He shrugged his shoulders and ever so slowly and laboriously

came down the iron ladder to the ground. I told the shore squad
to grab him and take him up to the diving hut and lock him
inside. They had barely left with a near-unconscious Murphy
when I heard shouting some distance in front of the crane. The
crane banksman came running up to me.

'Bob,' he called, 'Ian Alexander has fallen off the bulldozer
and his machine has gone down the slope into the sea.'

'What about Ian, is he all right?' I asked.

'He's fine but . . .' his voice trailed away.

Now it so happened that I knew Murphy and Ian were drinking
buddies, so I said, 'He's drunk and that's why he fell off the bulldozer, right?'

The banksman nodded his head in agreement.

I now had to have two more men grab hold of Ian and march
him away to the diving hut to join Murphy. If the boss got wind
of this, they would both be paid off instantly and I felt I must
save them from themselves.

The biggest job of all now faced Sandy. He had to tackle the
dangerous task of placing a heavy wire on the bulldozer, so we
could drag her back to the surface up the sloping face of the red
blaize. I stayed where I was on the inside of the piles and waited
for Sandy to come around the lead pile and up the sloping face.
The danger lay in the thought that perhaps the bulldozer had
not slid all the way down to the hard standing of the bottom
and might start sliding when Sandy was under it. It was a relief
when Sandy reported it was on the bottom. The shore squad
dropped Sandy a heaving line made fast to a heavy-duty wire
strop with a shackle on it. Sandy soon had everything made fast
and headed back towards the boat and out of harm's way. The
shore squad shackled the other end of the wire to the base of
the derrick and the relief driver took up the strain by reversing
the derrick back along her rails.

The bulldozer put up a fight by sinking into the face of the red blaize but she was no match for the strength of the mighty steam derrick and she was dragged groaning inexorably back to the surface and further up the slope, until she was back on level, compacted ground – the ground she herself had firmed up, to take the weight of the derrick, which had now saved her from a watery grave.

The following day was Friday and in the morning the night shift were complaining bitterly about the state of the diving hut. The two drunk men, locked inside for most of the night, had been violently sick all over the inside of the drying room. This was the room used by the linesmen to hang up and dry the diving suits after they had scrubbed them down with fresh water to rid them of salt. Things went from bad to worse that morning as Eric, Sandy and I had an argument regarding the fact that I could not hold an arc to burn the bottom holes for the tie rods. The trouble was an eight-foot high swell, which penetrated down to forty feet and caused us to sway back and forth, making it impossible to keep steady enough to burn the holes. Sandy suggested he had a solution and Eric pounced on it saying, 'I don't care how you manage it so long as you don't hold the piling men back, what's your idea anyway?'

Sandy looked at me and said, 'Suppose you lie flat on your belly and I lie on top of you, with one arm either side of you and I have a 56lb weight in each hand. Do you think you could hold an arc then?'

'It sounds real Heath Robinson to me Sandy, but it's crazy enough to maybe work.'

'Try it,' said Eric in an exasperated tone. 'Try Sandy's idea, go down and try it *now*; you have nothing to lose and I have everything to gain. Go down and try it.'

This was one of the things I liked about Sandy. He would try anything and sometimes he came up with some outlandish ideas but on the other hand sometimes they actually worked. So it proved on this occasion. I lay flat out on the bottom, opposite the burning jig, with the torch in my right hand. I was swaying from one side to the other, not violently but enough to make sure it was impossible to hold an arc. Sandy stretched out on my back and our helmets came together. He lifted both of his arms, one on each side of me, holding a 56lb weight in each hand clear of the bottom and I heard him say, 'Try it now!' without hitting his chin switch. With the helmets touching, the sound was conducted through without the diver phone.

I won't pretend it was easy but he did stabilise me sufficiently to hold an arc and burn the holes. We progressed from one to another and although we had a few blow-backs, we got the job done.

We always finished early on a Friday, which was pay day, and we had finished before the normal stopping time of 5 p.m. I went ashore on the dam to collect my sub. Sandy and the lads took the boat back to the old harbour. When I walked into the office, Frank was paying out subs to a queue of men. I waited until he had them all paid.

'Can I have my twenty pounds now?' I asked him.

'I don't think so,' he said, and I thought, this has got to be some kind of a joke.

I said, 'My mate Sandy will be waiting for me, can I have my money Frank?'

'I didn't put you through for a sub,' he said with a twisted look on his face.

Now I knew this was no joke and I could feel real anger welling up inside me. I turned away and walked out of the office. Sandy was waiting for me on the green across the road. I walked across to him and as I did so I realised that Frank had kept me standing there the full time it took him to pay out all the subs to the labourers and the piling crews. I felt a red mist come up before my eyes.

'Hang on a minute Sandy,' I said, 'I'll be right back.'

I turned back towards the office and saw Frank coming out and locking up. I walked up to him and with his usual sneer he said, 'What do you want now?'

I grabbed him by the neck, taking shirt, tie and most of the skin across the front of his throat in my right hand and shook the hell out of him.

'If you ever try making a fool out of me again you bastard, I will put you in hospital for a long time with a badly burst-up body.'

I was shouting into a face that was turning blue as he strangled in my grip.

A quiet voice behind me said, 'Are you annoyed about something Bob?'

It was my boss Eric. I let go of Frank and he fell to the ground, choking and spluttering.

'I most certainly am,' I answered.

Eric spoke in the same quiet tone as before. 'Come into the office in the morning Bob and we'll sort it out.'

I could feel my anger leaving me slowly and I said, 'Right Mr Hume, I'll do that,' and I marched away.

As I did so I heard Eric say to Frank behind me, 'You would be better advised to be careful in your dealings with these divers, they are all hard, wild men.'

26

The White Elephant

The dam was progressing towards the old harbour and the Overseas Divers' end was coming to meet up with us. There was still quite a distance between us but already we could feel the effects of the incoming tide accelerating, as it was forced to fill the whole bay through the steadily decreasing gap between our respective ends. One of the main problems was the shifting of the sandy bottom, which was now being moved inexorably towards the gap with the flow tide and then built up as the ebb tide brought some of it back. We had become used to finding the bottom waling roughly two feet above the seabed, because we were running parallel with the shoreline. Now we were finding difficulty in clearing the sand out of our way to get down to the proper level. At first we used small six-inch diameter air lifts, which can shift a surprising amount of sand, but eventually even they were no use.

The Overseas Divers had the same problem as ourselves and as a consequence the diving work slowed down considerably and held the whole job back. Eric called a crisis meeting to discuss the problem and he invited my big mate Sandy to attend as well. Now this was really sensible, for Sandy was the oldest and the most experienced diver on the job.

On entering Eric's office we found the boss and Matchet poring over a drawing. I recognised the drawing immediately, it was the Wimpey test bore report that Tom Black had shown us before the job started. Eric stabbed at the drawing with one finger, drawing our attention to it.

'According to this, where we are at the moment, the seabed should be at least four feet lower than it actually is.' He had a worried look on his face as he continued, 'There's no way we can bring the job in on time at the present rate of progress, so we must find a way to clear the sand faster. I'm open to any ideas.'

'We could make bigger air lifts on site,' said Sandy. Matchet shook his head saying, 'Too slow Sandy, I think we must hire in a sand sucking barge.'

I threw in my support of my mate. 'If we make bigger air lifts like Sandy suggests, then it will be anything but slow.'

'This will only be a temporary hold up anyway,' Sandy said.

Eric's face cleared somewhat but he said, 'If Wimpey's soundings are the same all the way, how can it be temporary Sandy?'

'Wimpey's soundings won't be wrong,' Sandy said. 'It's the tide race that's building the sand up, but in the next two or three hundred yards or so, we'll get a complete reversal and be dealing with a scour, which will leave the bottom waling away high above our heads.'

Matchet turned his back on Sandy and me and said to Eric, 'I think you should allow me to order in a sand sucking barge to get the job moving again.'

Eric gave in and said resignedly, 'OK Al you go ahead and get us a barge.'

The sand sucking barge arrived, with two men on board to operate it. It could only take ten tons of sand on board before it had to be towed away out into the Firth of Forth and emptied. It left a series of potholes in the bottom, which the tide promptly filled up again, and only reduced the overall level by approximately a few inches. We were forced to continue using our little six-inch diameter air lifts to get down low enough to place the bottom tie rods and walings.

One day I was kneeling in the trench Sandy and I had blown out of the bottom and was starting to cut the holes for the rods, when I noticed a large female partan crab lying in the bosom of the pile I was cutting. The red glare of my arc lit up the bottom all around and I saw a much smaller male crab make advances towards her and promptly climb on her back. The action of the pair took my attention off the arc I was holding and the torch gave a sudden vicious blow-back, which caused a globule of molten metal to be spat from the end of the burning rod. It takes two or three seconds for sea water to extinguish molten metal globules coming from a torch because they are five times hotter than molten lava. Enough time for it to drop, still glowing, on to the back of my sexy little friend. He literally flew off the top of his girlfriend and vanished into the surrounding darkness. I have often wondered if he told any of his pals about the red-hot momma he met that day.

Three weeks later, at finishing time, Sandy and I were climbing up onto the dam, and standing above us was Eric, with a face like thunder.

'You said the problem with the sand would be a temporary thing,' he stormed at Sandy. 'I'm paying a hundred pounds a day for that barge, plus two men's wages, and two tugs to tow it about.'

'That's not our fault,' Sandy answered loudly. 'You wouldn't listen to Bobby and I, when we told you we could make a big air lift on site. Instead, you decided to go with Mr Matchet and bring in that white elephant of a stupid barge.'

Eric controlled his anger with difficulty. 'Do you really believe you can shift more sand with an air lift than the barge can suck up?'

'We'll shift ten times the amount the barge will,' Sandy said, 'and permanently out of our way, with a big enough air lift.'

'Right let's do it. What do you need from me?' Eric's voice was now back to its normal, quiet tone.

'Contact Balfour Beattie and hire their sixty-foot high air lift reservoir and two Rolls Royce compressors. We'll get Fred the fitter to make the airlift on site.'

Eric's eyes widened. 'What do you mean you'll get rid of the sand permanently?' he asked.

Sandy pointed towards the far off shoreline.

'We'll blow it inside the dam, out of our way and towards the shoreline.'

'Where are you going to get all the power from?' Eric asked.

'We'll harness the power of the deep,' I said. 'We'll be working in forty to sixty feet of water, that's twenty to thirty pounds of pressure per square inch, by itself, and coupled with the volume of the reservoir we'll have more power than we really need.'

At last we managed to persuade Eric we could do it.

Fred made a beautiful job of the air lift, to Sandy's design that I drew from his own description. It was an eighteen-inch diameter steel pipe, ten feet long up to a thirty degree bend with a four foot extension beyond the bend and culminated in a long, heavy-duty corrugated hose. An air delivery apron was built into its lower end about two feet up from its intake and this was fed by two three-inch diameter hoses, one on either side. Welded to its outside were two sets of handles, one set three feet up, and one set eight feet up for the operators to hang on to. I must confess I had grave misgivings when I first saw it hanging on the derrick and being lowered to the bottom. Sandy and I were fully dressed and ready to give it its first go. We had a large audience on the dam head, which worried me. Sandy Green stood there, with two of his bosses. Beside them were Eric and Matchet and behind the front group were all the men of the shore and piling squads.

I had Buncer call up to the banksman to continue lowering away until she just took the bottom and no more. At the same time I whispered quietly to Sandy, 'Listen mate, are you sure we're going to be able to control that beast? I've never ever worked with an air lift anywhere near that size.'

'Neither have I,' Sandy said in a matter of fact way. 'But I think we'll be able to hang on to it.'

I almost had a fit, there and then. I had drawn the monster to Sandy's specification, thinking he had worked with something similar in the past. Now he was more or less admitting he did not know if we would be able to control it. To make matters worse, the Overseas men had now joined the audience above us, to watch our first attempt.

'Oh Sandy,' I groaned, 'I love a trier but this time I think you've pleased me too much. If it blows us both to the surface, we'll be the laughing stock of the whole job.'

'You worry too much,' Sandy said. 'As long as you just crack the air valve open and no more, we should be fine.'

'I have no intention other than to give her the absolute minimum flow of air to begin with until I see what's going to happen,' I replied.

The large air reservoir had been mounted on the bogey wagon carrying the back ballast of the sheer leg derrick and the shore squad informed us the compressors had built its pressure up to the maximum. There was no going back now. We finished dressing in turn and slipped down to the bottom.

Oh God, I thought, standing there in the dull misty red of the water, which barely allowed me to see the shadowy form of

Sandy standing beside me. It would have to be murky. We set off together, aided by Buncer's voice. 'Left a bit, left a bit more, steady, OK. Straight ahead, straight ahead, bear right a touch, now straight ahead, now steady as you go and you're there.'

Out of the gloom the monstrosity appeared. I spun my exhaust valve wide open and my helmet bore down on my shoulders. I lay down on the bottom and gripped hold of the control handles. 'Is your exhaust wide open?' Sandy asked above me. I chinned the buzzer.

'You better believe it,' I replied. 'We'll both have to be as heavy as possible to have any chance of controlling this big bitch.'

'Buncer?' Sandy said. 'Stand by to lower away.'

'Standing by to lower away Sandy.'

The man who had said 'you worry too much' before we left the boat now said, 'For God's sake Bobby just crack it open and no more.' His worried tone did not exactly inspire me with confidence as I eased open the accelerator. The hiss of the incoming air was clearly heard and the huge air lift began bouncing up and down violently. As suddenly as the bouncing had started, it stopped and the air lift took a savage bite out of the bottom.

'Lower away!' Sandy called.

'Lower away it is,' Buncer answered, and we were off. Within seconds the water around us cleared, as if by magic, and I could see the sand hurtling up through the air lift, with a violence I could never have envisaged. Sandy's boots were left hanging in open water as the sand fell away from his feet.

'Is it OK Bobby?' he asked.

'Fine Sandy, lower away as fast as you want,' I answered.

In minutes we were down to the bedrock and Sandy called for heave up and jib down at the same time. Buncer came on the phone asking if he could speak.

'Go ahead,' I answered.

'The boss is asking how it's going.'

I looked at the sides of the trench we were digging and estimated we were around fifteen to twenty feet down through the sand. The walls of the trench were continuing to run into the bottom at high speed and vanishing up the pipe with tremendous velocity. 'Just tell him it's going fine,' I said.

Sandy kept us moving forward all the time but it was still a surprise when we got the call that the derrick was flat out horizontal and could not take us any further without jibbing right up and travelling forward on its rails. So ended the first use of Sandy's mammoth air lift, which we christened 'Big Bertha'.

It was a tremendous success, except for one thing – the top handles were no use, because Sandy had been left hanging on to them with no place to stand as the sand was swept out from under his feet. We used it again the following day and I suppose it was really my fault as regards what happened.

The derrick had been moved forward on its rails a considerable distance and we were set to tackle a virgin area of the bottom. We were ready to repeat the exact method of the day before, with me lying on my belly and hanging on to the lower handles and Sandy gripping the high-level handles. Unfortunately I did not use the same caution as I had the day before when starting her up. As a result I opened up the accelerator more than just cracking it. The violent bouncing up and down was far greater than yesterday's effect. It almost tore itself free of my grip but it did tear itself out of Sandy's hands.

Sandy came sliding down the wall of the trench, unable to stop himself, and the first I knew of this was when his boots flew out underneath the mouth of the air lift. His midriff was immediately sucked up solidly against the air lift's mouth, shutting off the flow of sand and water and instantly filling the air lift with highly compressed air. It all happened so quickly I had no time to shut off the air flow before the handles were forcibly torn out of my grip and both Sandy and the air lift took off upwards like a space rocket.

'Emergency!' I called loudly. 'Take up Sandy's lines and pull hard on them. I'm coming back towards the boat so take up my slack.'

I was not going to remain where I was, in case 'Big Bertha' spilled all her air and thundered back to the bottom. I scrambled up the slope towards the boat as fast as I could go and as I did so Buncer came on the phone.

'Everything's OK,' he said, 'we have Sandy on the ladder.'

'What happened?' I asked.

'Bobby, you should have seen this,' Buncer said excitedly. 'Big Bertha surfaced and cleared the water completely, and spat Sandy out, like a killer whale tossing a sealion in the air.'

'Is he OK?'

'He seems to be, we just took his helmet off, but he's very white in the face.'

Back on board the boat I apologised to Sandy, who was obviously shaken by the experience. I also said, 'I'm glad it didn't happen yesterday when we had all that crowd watching us.'

Sandy's brows came down and he thrust out his lower jaw in a threatening manner, as he scowled up at me saying bitterly, 'Oh! So it was OK to do it to me today, just because there was no bastard up there to see it.'

I had to laugh at the very idea that I did it deliberately because there was nobody up top to see it. The white face cleared immediately and slowly gave way to a smile, and once more his large eyes crinkled and then danced with merriment.

27

Big Bertha

We discovered it was easier for one man to work with Big Bertha on his own, provided he handled the accelerator with care, and kept his body well back from her mouth. We also devised a cut-off valve to be operated by the shore squad in an emergency. The need for this became apparent when I was working down through the bottom one day and Bertha slammed against something flat and took off for the surface like she had done previously with Sandy. I raced back towards the boat, up the sloping side of the trench I had just dug. 'Take up my lines!' I called, 'and take me away.'

Back on board the diving boat the lads told me Bertha had once more cleared the surface in a spectacular leap and spat out what they thought was a railway wagon, before she and the strange object had sunk back below the surface once more.

'A railway wagon?' I said, and laughed. 'You have to be joking.'

'We saw it clearly,' Billie said, 'and that's what it looked like didn't it Buncer?'

Buncer nodded in agreement.

'It was very small,' he said, 'but it *looked* just like a railway wagon – it had four wheels, the same as a railway wagon.'

I called up to the shore squad to cut the air off at the reservoir and take Bertha up on the dam head. 'OK boys, throw that helmet on me and I'll find out what the hell it is. Buncer, see if you can talk me close to where you last saw it, before it sank.'

Back on the bottom Buncer guided me straight to the strange object, lying on its side close to the hole Bertha had dug. Sure enough it was a miniature wagon designed to run on rails. It was approximately four feet long and about two feet six inches wide and three feet deep. It was built out of solid oak planks, more than two inches thick, and although the timber was as black as coal, it was remarkably well preserved. There was no sign of rust on the axles or the little wheels, which spun easily when I moved them. I realised it must have been buried in the sand for possibly hundreds of years, for Bertha had hit it more than fifteen feet down from the seabed. Somehow I felt the little curiosity of a wagon was an important find and should be handled very carefully. I had a large rock pan delivered to the bottom and then slung the small wagon onto the pan still lying on its side, rather than on its wheels. I then returned to the boat and had my helmet removed. I called up to the banksman to tell the crane driver to bring it up slowly and stop it just above the surface and allow all the water to drain out of the rock pan before lifting it onto the dam head.

Once it was safely landed on the dam, I had the shore squad hose it down with plenty of fresh water and then dry it thoroughly with bolts of sackcloth. I climbed up on the dam to view the result and we finished the job by smearing all the metalwork with motor grease. The following afternoon we had a visit from three men from the Edinburgh Museum, accompanied by Eric. They studied the wagon for a considerable time and then gave us its history.

Around about two hundred years ago it was the common practice to employ very young boys and young girls to push these little bogeys into tunnels running straight into Preston

Links colliery. Once they had been filled with small coal, their job was to push them out again via separate tunnels, with a very slight downgrade to assist them with the loaded wagons. These young children were recruited from nearby orphanages and paid a mere pittance for their hard labour. Both boys and girls wore nothing but short trousers and all of them were bare-footed. To the present day, that little bogey resides in the Edinburgh Mining Museum.

On any one day working with Big Bertha, the seabed surrounding the excavated area would finish up covered with the most amazing variety of shells. There were scallop shells as big as soup plates, oyster shells the same size, razor-fish shells twelve inches long and two inches broad. Among the well-known shell-fish remains of giant clams, enormous cockles and mussels there were also conch shells, as big as any found in tropical waters. It dawned on me that the sea animals of thousands of years ago must have prospered greatly by mankind's inability to harvest the deep waters. The oldest shells were so badly abraded by the action of the sand that they were milky white in colour and paper thin, so thin they almost allowed light through them like glass.

One Sunday afternoon I had just shut Big Bertha down and sent her back up to the dam head after clearing the area between the two lines of piles. The sea was quite still in there, although a fair old swell was laying up against the seaward piles. The diving boat lay at anchor inside the bay, sheltered from the worst of the swell.

'OK Buncer,' I said, 'take up my lines, I'm coming back towards the lead pile.'

I knew the boat was around the inside so they could not see my bubbles.

'Taking up the slack Bobby,' Buncer answered.

I set off towards the lead pile, which I would have to go around before they would see me coming. Suddenly I was slammed helmet first into the bottom with tremendous force. My helmet was buried in the sand and my boots were now higher than my exhaust valve. I could feel my legs beginning to inflate and I pedalled furiously to sink my legs into the sand. I had a vision of myself turning completely upside down and being rendered helpless. In sheer desperation I heaved on my lines and arched my back. The helmet came up slightly then stuck fast. Luckily it was enough, and my air exhaust valve was just high enough to vent my legs once more. The immediate danger over I concentrated on digging my legs deeper into the soft sand, for it was impossible to free my helmet.

'What the hell fell on me?' I asked.

'We can't see you from here,' Buncer answered, 'has something fallen on you?'

'I don't know what it is but it's very heavy and it has taken my lines down into the sand.'

'Sandy is aboard, do you need him down?' Buncer sounded concerned.

'Hang fire,' I said, 'until I suss this one out. I don't want to bring Sandy down until I find out what hit me.'

All the time I was talking I was digging down through the sand with both hands following my lines. It must have taken me almost ten minutes before I came upon a tie rod pinning my lines to the bottom. The half-ton tie rod was lying at an angle and it had taken my lines down into the sand about three feet. I began working my lines slowly up the slope until they cleared the sand and came free. I was now able to stand up and I realised one end of the rod was still resting through the inner piles. It was obviously one of our own bottom rods and the groundswell must have slowly moved it along until it came out of the seaward piles and dropped to the seabed, hitting my lines about four feet away from my helmet.

Phew! I thought as I ducked under the rod, on my way back to the boat. That was a close call, that 10 hundredweight rod had fallen about fifteen feet and another two steps towards the lead pile and it would have landed smack on my helmet. Lady Luck had favoured me once more that afternoon.

28

A Dead Suit

It became a day I would remember for the rest of my life and would prove that one man's frustration and aggravation can so affect others that simple mistakes can be made, to the danger of life and limb. My speaker, in the top of my helmet, had begun acting up and was making and breaking all morning. From it came a stuttering, stammering unintelligible garble of broken words, mixed with spells of normal speech. I was not really bothered by it, for I was now welding the sealing plates on the midwater tie rods, those that the top squads could no longer reach as the depth steadily increased. This meant I required very little communication with the surface, whereas Sandy needed the phone constantly while pitching tie rods in the foremost section, well away from me. He was obviously struggling in shifting sand and the air was blue with his constant cursing and swearing. I moved along the bottom until I was underneath the next rod and, closing my spindle valve for a few seconds, I inflated a bit and then leapt upwards. I sailed up about twelve feet from the bottom and grabbed hold of the rod. I swung one leg over it and drew myself closer to the pile it passed through.

'Ok,' I said, 'pass me down the welding torch.' There was no answer. In my helmet, Sandy's voice was rising in pitch.

'For God's sake tell that driver to slew east *now*.'

I waited a few minutes but the tirade continued. 'Tam! I said up a wee bit, AW THIS IS RIDICULOUS. HOLD IT, I SAID HOLD IT!'

'All held Sandy,' said Tam in a very worried voice.

'IT'S STILL MOVING TAM, IT'S NOT ALL HELD!'

'The banksman says it's all held Sandy.'

I was beginning to feel sorry for poor Tam.

'The bloody thing was still swinging after you said it WAS ALL HELD!'

Sandy was shouting at the top of his voice. If anything it was an improvement when my speaker began shutting down in fits and starts until it finally gave up altogether.

'Send the welding torch down,' I repeated.

Again there was no answer and worse was to follow. My incoming air suddenly took a noticeable dip. I immediately pushed home my spindle and closed my exhaust valve by a couple of turns.

'What's happening to my air?' I enquired, nervously by now. Still no answer, then I was given a sudden fright with the first thud of the Delmag piling hammer starting up.

A breath-catching thought came into my head: what if they had dropped a pile on top of my lines, which were around the lead pile and they were now driving them into the bottom? Logic prevailed and I realised I was still getting air, albeit in a reduced amount. Hardly had I recovered from my first thought, when my air supply took another dip. Again I screwed in my exhaust valve another turn, and demanded loudly, 'What in the name of God is going on up there, what is happening to my air supply!'

There was no response from the boat, perhaps they could not hear me. I was now beginning to feel real fear, something that I had never experienced in my life before. I took hold of my lines and gave an attention pull; all I got was more of my lines coming down to me. For the rest of my life I would feel thankful for my next decision, for I decided to inflate slightly and drop down to the bottom, so I could tug seriously on my lines to demand attention.

I did this and I gave my lines a mighty heave, which only resulted in more coming down beside me. It was at that moment that my air stopped altogether and I quickly screwed my exhaust valve hard down.

'Surface!' I called. 'What are you trying to do to me. WHAT'S HAPPENING TO MY AIR SUPPLY?'

I cannot adequately describe the sound of my own voice reverberating around the inside of an otherwise silent helmet or the intenseness of the silence that followed. I gripped hold of my lines with both hands and began to follow them back out towards the boat. To add to my mental turmoil, my brain was screaming, 'twenty minutes to half an hour a "dead suit" can keep a hard hat man alive as long as it does not crush him first'. Then I looked out of my right light and saw the considerable flow of small bubbles coming from my completely closed exhaust valve. It was usually a diver's own responsibility in those days to maintain the most important parts of his equipment. Those were the non-return valves of the air intake and the air exhaust valve. My non-return air intake valve was performing perfectly but my air exhaust valve was leaking badly.

I was in a very real danger of being crushed to death and nobody up above seemed to care. I could not believe how much line I pulled down from that boat before it tightened up enough for me to brave the climb.

If I should get more than halfway up and be allowed to drop back to the bottom, then I was a dead man. I climbed with that fear in my head until I reached the boat and swung onto the diving ladder. There I saw the strangest sight. Sandy sat in the

215

stern sheets with his blood-red face cupped in badly swollen hands. His sparse but long hair lay straggling down the left side of his face, leaving the top of his head completely bald. Normally Sandy would have it covering the baldness and held there by whatever strong glue he used as hair cream. Somehow his normal appearance always suggested one of the singing barbers to me, but not today. Sandy looked hellish.

Tam Sutherland was standing before him with a mournful look on his face, as if all that was happening was his fault. Billie Manclark was the only man who saw me arrive on the ladder and showed surprise at my sudden appearance. His wide-eyed look was one of horror as I tapped my front light with one finger to show him I wanted it removed. Damn me if Billie did not ignore me and instead of removing the glass he began frantically hauling up my loose lines from the seabed. I was now panting with short shallow breaths and the dead suit clung to my body with a feeling of rigidity, as if it was made of tin. There was also considerable heat building up in my helmet and I could feel a cold clammy sweat break out on my forehead.

I felt the first symptoms of dizziness and deliberately stepped into the cockpit with a crash, still jabbing at my glass with my finger. The noise alerted Tam who grabbed the toggle bar and unscrewed my glass.

The hot foul air exploded outwards in Tam's face as I gasped, 'Turn on my air.'

He reached the air panel and as I watched he made the mistake of turning the air off from Sandy's discarded helmet lying in the bottom of the boat. He came back towards me and I tried to calm him down by gasping quietly, 'Tam, be a good lad and turn on my air, before I suffocate in here.'

I will never forget the look on his face as he rushed back to the panel and at last turned on my air. I motioned to him to increase the flow and he did. I wanted a good blow to clear my head before removing my helmet.

When it came to working out just exactly what went so hope-lessly wrong, we were faced with not so much of a comedy of errors but rather the sweetest collection of mistakes brought about by the sheer panic of our inexperienced handlers, due to the exas-peration of Sandy with the derrick driver. He had worked himself up into a frenzy and yet the derrick driver had done nothing wrong. Sandy had far too much slew on the crane but Tam did not tell him, only because Tam did not know. Sandy then called to have his air increased again and again, until the pump could not maintain the air reservoirs' working pressure of 200 pounds per square inch. The air tanks came down to fifty PPSI, and according to both Billie and Tam the noise of the air coming through the diver phone from Sandy's helmet was colossal.

They never noticed the central gauge on the diving panel steadily falling: every time they tried to increase Sandy's air, they were decreasing mine, due to the falling pressure of the reser-voirs.

Sandy finally made himself ill and gave up on the job, surfaced and climbed on board. Tam took his helmet off and laid it down on the deck. He then turned my air off, instead of Sandy's by mistake, and no one on board noticed the air howling out of the helmet at their feet. Looking back on the whole incident I am not sure whether or not my big mate suffered a small heart attack that day. I do know the crew were so concerned by the look of Sandy that I was forgotten altogether and I narrowly escaped death, by the closest of margins.

29

Skin Suit vs. Hard Hat

It was such a lovely morning, the September sun shining on a calm, unruffled sea. Sandy was still below taping up the ends of the tie rods. Like myself, he had been told it was coffee time but he had decided he would carry on for a bit longer. I sat in the stern of the *Eadie*, enjoying both the excellent mug of coffee and the warmth the September sun still retained. I was in no hurry to go back down and I asked Billie to fill my mug up again. I was fully dressed, except for front and back weights and my helmet, which lay at my feet. I was so much at peace with the world that I hardly noticed the discordant thudding of the five-ton Delmag piling hammer as it drove the piles down through the rock bottom, up ahead of us. I smiled to myself, as I listened to Sandy cursing and swearing like a cantankerous old man, every time he had to open a new roll of Denso tape. Nowadays the tape was sealed in, with the new plastic sealant, which I admit was a bitch to remove from the thick grease of the tape itself.

From above and behind me came the one and only thing designed to wreck my equanimity at that time. Matchet's voice.

'Bob, send one of your lads over in the dinghy to pick me up.'

Now, this was something new, he had never, ever, been on board any of the diving boats before. He had always aggravated us, by his interference in our work, from the distance of the dam.

'Billie,' I said quietly, 'take the boat and bring the bastard over.'

Matchet arrived in the dinghy and he had a sizeable parcel under his arm. He climbed on board and began opening up his parcel. From it he produced a brand-new neoprene wetsuit.

'Your lads can help me dress,' he said to me.

'Oh no they won't,' I said, 'there's no way I can let you go down there.'

'Look Bob I'm the general foreman on this job and I want to see what's being done underwater as well as above.'

'You have no Fitness Register and the law says you can't dive without one. I cannot allow you to go down.'

'Bob, you know as well as I that laws are made and broken every day, I'm going down with or without your help.'

'What the hell do you want to go down for anyway?'

'To see for myself that everything is being done properly.'

'The SSEB have a fully qualified diving inspector in Sandy Green, he checks our work regularly, if the electricity company are happy with it, why can't you accept it?'

'Bob, I just want to have a look. Now are your men going to dress me or not?'

'I told you, my men will not put you down, you don't have a phone, you don't have a doctor's certificate, if you drown down there we are all guilty of culpable homicide.'

'Aw, come on Bob, don't let us get all theatrical about this.'

He was steadily drawing the wet suit up around himself all the time we were arguing. He was without doubt the most ignorant and stubborn Irishman I ever came across. 'I could order your lads to help me dress.'

'They won't obey you, a linesman is trained to give the diver everything he wants except death.'

He fell silent, but kept dressing and clipped on a weight belt. One look told me it was too light for him but I said nothing.

'When you're working with your skin suits Bob, where do you attach your air line to your pump?'

I didn't answer him.

'I'll find it,' he said, and walked forward to the compressor room. He came back after about ten minutes, wearing a new normal air mask, and climbed over the side. His frog flippers thrashed around for a bit and at last he sank out of sight. We watched his bubbles travelling along the face of the piles.

'Hey Bob,' Sandy said over the phone, 'are you still on the boat?'

'I am Sandy,' I answered.

'What the hell is this bastard doing down here?'

'It's a long story, I'll tell you when you come up.'

Sandy had made a real fool of Matchett about a month prior to that day. We were finishing a shift and climbed up on the dam where we met Eric with Matchet who were looking at a tie rod at their feet.

'It happens sometimes,' said the Irishman. 'A nut jams and nothing on earth will shift it and you just have to scrap the whole rod. See all the torn metal on the rod, well that's where the chain grips held on while we tried to unscrew the nut, but it was impossible.'

Sandy stopped and said quietly, 'I'll take the nut off for you.'

'It can't come off Sandy,' Matchet said aggressively. Sandy ignored him and turned to Eric. 'I can't save the nut but you'll be able to use the rod again.'

Eric said, 'Go ahead Sandy.'

I was about to learn from my big mate, as he dragged over a burner's barrow. Now if Matchet had only shut his big mouth, he would not have put his foot in it, but no. He had to blurt out, 'That never works Sandy, the thread of the rod always melts and that's it, finished.' Sandy paid no attention to him and lit the sapphire torch and adjusted the oxygen flow. He knelt beside the rod and, turning the torch horizontal, he applied it across the width of the seven-inch diameter nut on its extreme edge only. He cut down to roughly halfway towards the thread. He brought the torch back up to the edge and again cut down making a V-shaped cut that went halfway down again. At no time did the torch come anywhere near the thread of the rod. He switched off the torch and picked up a burner's slag hammer. A series of small taps with the hammer and the huge nut spun effortlessly off the rod. This was something I had never seen done before.

'Where did you learn that Sandy?' Eric asked.

'That's one of the first things you're taught, when you first start working with walings and tie rods,' my big mate said nonchalantly.

The waling and tie rod expert said nothing.

After Matchet surfaced and had Billie take him back to the dam, I got on the phone to the east end. Tony Sparrow answered and I told him what had happened, to warn him that Matchet was on his way over. The overseas divers shared the same view as ourselves, where Matchet was concerned, but there was a difference – after all, theirs was a separate sub-contract.

What happened next was told to me by Geoff Kane while we were having a few drinks together several days later.

'I was working below when you phoned Tony. He came on the blower and told me how the Irishman came poking his nose in where he was not welcome so I was ready for him. I was bolting up the waling fishplates when I felt a tap on my shoulder and looking round I saw the clown goggling at me and making all sorts of stupid thumbs up signs with both hands. I grabbed him around the middle and turned him upside down and stuffed him head first between the piles and the waling, jamming his arms solid to his sides. I then carried on with my job.'

'My God Geoff, you could have drowned him, being upside down, it would only take a small amount of water in a face mask to drown a man.'

'I kept looking under the waling at him, every now and then, just in case he was drinking too much seawater for the good of his health and he kept staring back at me with eyes sticking out like a dog's bollocks. I put the fear of fucking death into the bastard before I dragged him back out again. He flew back to the surface at a rate of knots. I reckon I got the message across to him that on the seabed, the skin suit man versus the hard hat is strictly a no contest.'

Matchet never again came back for another underwater look.

30

Sandy Packs Up

It was on a Thursday afternoon and I was at home in bed and fast asleep, prior to going on night shift. Dod and I were back as a team and Sandy and Ian were covering the day shift at Cockenzie. My wife Mabel came into the bedroom and woke me up.

'Sandy McGill is standing in the street shouting up to our window.'

'What does he want?' I asked, noting the time on my bedside cabinet: the clock showed it was ten minutes past one in the afternoon.

'He wants to speak to you but he won't come up the stairs.'

'Tell him I'm getting up and tell him to come up to the house.'

I dressed and hurried through to the living room. The front window was open and Mabel said, 'He won't come up,' and she gestured towards the open window.

I looked out and saw Sandy standing in the street below me.

'What's going on mate?' I asked.

'I've jacked in,' he said simply.

'Come up to the house,' I said.

'No, I'm going home, I'm not coming up.' And he turned and began to walk away, still looking up at me. I was becoming exasperated by his strange agitated manner.

'Sandy,' I said, 'what do you mean you've jacked it in? What happened to make you pack in a hundred pounds a week job. I would sweep the streets for that kind of money.'

'It was that bastard Matchet,' he said, stopping and turning around.

'What's he done now, what could he possibly do to make you pack up?'

'I was sitting fully dressed on the *Eadie*, waiting for the piling squad to finish pitching piles, so I could have the derrick. He came along and shouted down to me, "Sandy, one of our bosses is coming on the job, so put your helmet on and go down." I told him I would not go down just to blow bubbles for no man, and we got into an argument.'

'Sandy why did you not ignore him and tell him to take it up with me?'

'Because he ordered me to go down and I said I would go down only when I had a job to do. He then said, "Well Sandy what are you going to do." I was so angry I said, "I would jack first before I would go underwater just to blow bubbles to fool one of the firm's bosses." With a sneer on his face he said, "Well Sandy that is up to you, so do you want me to tell Frank you are packing up?" And I was so wild I said, "You do that."'

'Oh Sandy,' I said sadly, 'you have left me with no argument at all.'

'Maybe so Bobby,' Sandy said, as once more he began walking away. 'But it was all because of that big ignorant get of an Irishman suckering me into packing up.'

The following Monday Dod and I were back on day shift and now we were joined by Ian Crow, who could not dive at night by himself. So now we had lost not only Sandy but also the whole night shift, until such time as we could find another experienced diver to team up with Ian. I also had to find work for the rest of the previous week's night shift boat crew, so I gave Dod and Ian the work in hand, while I tried to work it out. I had already determined I would have a showdown with Matchet, and to that end, I had arranged a meeting with Eric for later that morning.

At ten o'clock I knocked on Eric's office door and on entering I found Matchet already there. During a rather preliminary heated debate between Matchet and myself, Eric sat silent, obviously absorbing each of our arguments. I had the feeling of getting the better of the Irishman to start with by bringing up the clashes of personalities theory. Matchet then changed tactics and, controlling his Irish temper, he became an obsequious smiling rat.

'Aw come on Bob, I can't stop a man from packing up, if that is what he wants to do.'

'You goaded him into it, by ordering him underwater, when there was no work for him to go at. Did you stop to think of the responsibilities of Mr Hume here, trying to keep this contract on time and seriously short of qualified underwater men? No, you did not, and as a result we lost the most experienced diver on the job.'

Eric spoke for the first time, in his soothing, quiet manner.

'As Al said Bob, he can't stop a man from leaving our employment, if that is what he wants to do.'

Matchet put on his smarmy voice.

'There was nothing I could do to stop him Bob.'

'That is not true, you pulled him onto a sucker punch when he said he would not go under water just to blow bubbles to fool a boss into thinking he was working down below.'

I picked up the quick sideways glance Eric threw at Matchet.

'And when you asked him what he was going to do and he answered he would jack first, you quickly said you would tell Frank to make up his books.'

Eric's eyes flashed again in Matchet's direction.

I now tried to press home my advantage by saying, 'Dolphins and whales are safe underwater through aeons of years of evolution, man is not and you came across an honest man, who refused to pretend to be working to fool a boss and you jumped at the chance to get rid of him because your personalities clashed.'

'Not true Bob,' Matchet lied. 'I quite liked Sandy and I was sorry to see him go.'

This was an obvious blatant lie so I leapt in, before he could back out.

'Oh! So you would be happy to see him back, and the twenty-four-hour day and night shift diving teams working again.'

Eric noticed the slight hesitation before Matchet said unhappily, 'Of course I would like to see him back and the two shifts working again.'

'Right Al,' I said, 'I will bring him back and re-establish the two shifts again and let us try working with a bit more harmony and Mr Hume will see his contract gain time and be a happier man.'

I too knew how to use a bit of smarm when necessary.

'Will he come back Bob?' Eric asked.

'He will for me,' I answered.

'Now that's settled Al, I wonder if you could leave Mr Hume and I alone for a bit as I want to discuss something to do with Sandy, which must remain completely confidential.'

Matchet looked aghast, I was dismissing him, the general foreman. I made it a bit easier for him, God only knows why. 'Nothing at all to do with you Al,' I said.

Eric rose saying, 'Thank you Al, I will speak to you later.' He was always the perfect gentleman.

After Matchet left the office, I said, 'Eric, Sandy cannot read or write, so with your permission, I want to write to his wife

Peggy and tell her to pretend the letter is from you, and you want to see him in your office. When he arrives, and believe me he will come down, I would like you to tell him you are too busy to see him but to go down to the job and see me, will you do that?'

'Yes I can do that but do you think he will come back to work for us?'

'He will,' I said. 'And maybe the bloody Irishman will stay off his back after this.'

Eric shook his head at my disparaging remark. 'I learned a few things from this meeting that I did not know before Bobby, but to tell you the truth, Mr Matchet is very well thought of by my boss.'

He raised his eyebrows as he escorted me to the door. I nodded my understanding and left him, as he quietly said, 'Bullshit baffles brains.'

During the next two days I kept a sixth man aboard the diving boat – Tam – and I told him what I wanted him to do when Sandy showed up.

'Tell him how desperate I am to get his help on this job and point out to him that you and the rest of his former team might be out of a job because we can't get a replacement diver.'

On the Thursday afternoon, I was sitting in the stern sheets of the *Eadie*, drinking a mug of coffee and again enjoying the sunshine. I stood up and asked Billie for a bottle. Tam soaped up my right wrist and assisted me to draw my right arm inside my suit and Billie passed the bottle down inside the rim of my corselet. I could now do what no lady could do and remain dry inside the suit, as I relieved myself. I now passed the half full bottle back out of my suit via the inside rim of the corselet. I had just managed to thrust my right arm back through its sleeve when we were told Sandy was on his way down to the boat. I climbed quickly onto the diving ladder and said to Billie, 'As soon as he arrives, be prepared to put my helmet on when I tell you to.'

Sandy appeared on the dam head and shouted aggressively, 'What the hell do you want?'

I said quietly to Billie, 'Put the helmet on,' but turned my head to Sandy and called up to him, 'Come aboard Sandy,' and on went my helmet. The dinghy was going over for my mate when I left the surface. I carried on with the job I was doing, tightening up tie rods on the bottom strake.

Sandy's voice came over the phone, 'What do you want Bobby?' but this time his tone was much sweeter.

'Hang on Sandy,' I said, 'I'll be up shortly.'

I deliberately carried on for some time to let Tam work on my big mate, then I surfaced.

When my helmet came off, Sandy was sitting in the stern, fully dressed in all his woollens and his red cap on. I had a hard job to stop myself from laughing at his first ludicrous question, which was, 'What do you want?'

I knew I dare not laugh as I said, 'I will tell you what I want. I want my mate to climb into that big suit and get himself down below to give me a hand with this bloody job.'

The following morning, a Friday, Frank came out of the offices carrying our Fitness Registers. 'Sorry lads,' he said as he handed them to us. 'I forgot to give you these last night, you both have to go for a medical this morning at eleven o'clock so you may as well set off right now.'

As we walked away across the green Sandy quipped, 'You know Bobby, that man's manner has really improved a long long way since you had a quiet word with him.'

We arrived at Dr Batter's surgery smack on eleven, only to be told Frank had made another mistake and our appointment was not until three. We were walking away and passing the Port of Leith bar, when Sandy said, 'Fancy a pint and a rum and peppermint?'

That was it, we passed the next three and a half hours in the pub and had a great time. Sandy had a high tolerance of alcohol and no one would know he had a real cargo on board, the only giveaway was the lustrous sheen that came over his eyes. I had an even higher tolerance of alcohol than Sandy at that time, so poor Dr Batters had no idea we were both drunk when we went through our medical. He was even delighted with our blood pressure reading saying, 'Very good lads, keep up the good work.' Three months later at our next medical, he was very angry and he said, 'This time I want a sample of urine, not a sample of Nelson's blood.'

Unfortunately it was the end of Sandy's diving days. The doctor refused to sign his Register saying, 'I am sorry Sandy, but I cannot allow you to carry on diving, you are in grave danger of a heart attack at any moment.'

Sandy stayed on the diving team, as our most experienced linesman and never dived again.

31

The Big Swim

Monday night, at seven o'clock, we left the old harbour to begin another week's night shift. Harmony had been restored on the job, now that Sandy was back on the day shift and working as linesman to Ian. Tonight, Dod would carry on wearing the standard dress and tackle all the work on the bottom. I would wear my Royal Naval Avon dry suit with normal air mask and flippers. My job would be bolting up the fishplates, tying the midwater walings together. A fair old swell was running as we passed the Overseas Divers' boat, lying at anchor off the east end of the job. There was no sign of life on board, as we swept by on our way to the west end. Buncer had the *Eadie* almost flat out and running before the swell; she rose and fell about four feet as she ploughed through the smooth-topped waves.

We steered inside the inner leaf of piles at our end of the job, and here the swell was reduced somewhat, being broken by the outer leaf of piles. We anchored and began dressing in our respective gear. Once fully dressed, I stood up and asked Billie to pass my weight belt around me. Billie looked at me blankly.

'I've forgotten it,' he said, 'I just knew something was missing but I couldn't think what it was.'

'Billie,' I said, 'there's no way I can get down there, without my body belt.'

'Do you want me to row over to the dam and walk ashore to get it?'

'No Billie, that would take you half the night.'

'Can we start up the boat and sail back to the old harbour and I'll walk from there?'

I pointed at Dod, almost completely dressed by that time.

'No Billie, that would mean Dod stripping everything off again before we could sail back to the harbour. By the time we got back here, he would have no chance of finishing his night's work.'

I thought for a minute or two and then said, 'It's less than a half mile to the east end, I'll swim over and get a loan of a belt from the Overseas boys.'

I had not vented my suit, so I had plenty of buoyancy and I set off swimming slowly, doing the lazy crawl. It was black dark out there but every time I lifted over the top of the swell, I could see the lights of the cluster lamps at the east end clearly. The heavens above me were twinkling with myriads of stars and the oily swell below me appeared to be blacker than the blackest of inks. I remember thinking how lucky I was, that I was not swimming in some foreign clime, with the threat of sharks or killer whales around. This train of thought did me no good, as it caused me to begin thinking of how closely I must resemble a seal. The smooth black Avon dry suit, with the flippers churning water behind me, the neoprene one-piece helmet covering my head in its entirety. Not just a seal, I thought, but a wounded seal forced to travel on the surface all the time. I began to imagine all sorts of sea creatures, which could be watching the surface from the dark depths beneath me. I did my best to control this idiotic fanciful imagery and dispel it from my mind but it clung on with the tenacity of a limpet on the face of a rock. At last I rounded the seaward piles and swam in towards the Overseas diving boat in calmer, quieter waters.

The boat lay in total darkness with no one on deck. I swam around it, to the diving ladder on the far side. I climbed up the ladder and could now see the faint blue night light inside the cabin. As I stepped aboard, something stirred in the cabin and a well-known voice said, 'Haw! What's this then, fucking spying on us eh!?'

It was Jack Sayers.

'I'm not spying on you Jack, my linesman forgot my waist belt and I came over to borrow one from you.'

'Did you swim over?' Jack said shaking his head in disbelief.

'I did,' I replied.

'Bob you must be crackers to swim that distance just for a belt, come in the cabin and get a heat.'

I not only stayed for a heat but also swallowed a steaming hot cup of coffee, as we spoke in whispers, so as not to disturb the young divers who were fast asleep. Jack told me his young team had attended a special do the night before and he was allowing them to sleep off the effects of the drink. He also told me he would have them up in plenty time to complete their work before the morning came in.

He then took me through to the weight belt bins and looking at me in an appraising manner, as if gauging my weight, he suggested thirty pounds.

I motioned higher.

'Thirty-five pounds?'

I raised one hand.

'Forty pounds?'

Again I upped the hand.

'Forty-five pounds?'

I nodded.

'You fat bastard,' Jack said, grinning at me as he handed me the belt. 'Are you really going to swim back wearing that?'

'I am Jack, and thanks for the loan of it.'

'It's too heavy for any of us Bob, so you keep it.'

I set off on the return journey and now I was feeling the extra weight. I now had to swim side-stroke as I no longer slipped easily over the top of the swell. Instead I burrowed into the water halfway up each trough and the peaks broke high over my head. Our cluster lamps appeared to take forever to come any nearer and I was blowing quite hard long before I swam into the quieter water on the shore side of the dam. I reached the diving ladder and clung onto the bottom rung until my breathing returned to normal. Billie stood above me looking very concerned.

'Are you all right Bob?' he asked.

'I will be Billie, in about an hour's time.'

I hauled myself up another two rungs and pulling the quick release tab on the belt I handed it up to Billie, and boy was I glad to get rid of it.

'My God!' said Billie, 'I was watching you all the way and you kept vanishing under the water with every wave and I kept thinking I was going to be responsible for you drowning out there.'

'Billie,' I said, 'I must confess, I have always been a very good swimmer all my life and I have swum some great distances in my time, but tonight was the hardest and most frightening swim I ever took on.'

Dod came aboard shortly after midnight and we settled down in the warmth of the cabin to have our mid-shift meal. The cabin smelled strongly of the bacon and eggs Buncer had been cooking before we came aboard. The food always tasted better after emerging from the cold water of the month of December. Buncer passed out our plates and then said, 'Manhole Heid has been kicking up holy murder and accusing us of holding up the piling squad.'

'He got annoyed because I would not give him the derrick,' Dod said, 'but I was not finished with it.'

'Quite right Dod,' I said. 'How many times has he hung onto it, when we were desperate for it?'

Buncer passed out the mugs of coffee saying, 'He was shouting down to the boat saying divers are a useless shower of buggers.'

In the morning, we all piled on board a bus, laid on by the company to take us all home to Edinburgh. On the way, Martin Donleavy started bitching about divers again and I said, 'My divers have more sense than a piling foreman who does not know the difference between driving a pile into rock and driving it into fresh air.'

'Stop the bus,' Martin called loudly, 'I'm going to knock your head off, Bobby Sinclair.'

'Right,' I said, 'stop the bus and let me see you try it.'

The bus driver pulled up and I jumped out the back door. If I was going to fight, I wanted room to move about in. I felt the onset of the red mist as Martin also jumped out the back door but to my surprise he said, 'Oh! This is nonsense Bobby, we've been friends for donkey's years. I don't want to fall out with you.'

He extended his right hand to shake hands. I made a point of showing him a left hand balled up into a threatening fist but also offered my right hand saying, 'Martin you are the man who offered me outside but if you still wish us to remain friends then fair enough.'

Meanwhile, while we spoke, Martin's eighteen-year-old son jumped out the side door of the bus and with a quick thumb action a seven-inch flick-knife opened in his hand. Dod leapt out behind him and said, 'Put that away or I will take it off you and I will ram it up your arse.'

The boy promptly closed the knife and put it away.

Two days later Buncer told me that after I had jumped out

the bus and Martin was following me out, Dod had said to him, 'You're a brave man.'

Donleavy had stopped and said, 'What do you mean?'

Dod had raised his eyebrows and said, 'You mean you don't know you're going up against an ex-Royal Naval boxing champion?'

Now that was not true, for I had lost my semi-final bout in Newcastle against the eventual final winner, a fellow Scot from Dundee called Steven Harris, in the year 1951. In that memorable semi-final I split open Steve's right eyebrow with a gash two inches long in the first round, but in those days they did not stop a bout because of blood-letting and to be honest, for the remainder of the bout, he showed me a bit of really superior left-hand work. So well had he worked me over that my girlfriend Mabel, my wife now, cried when she saw me and came back from a butcher's shop with raw steaks to put on my eyes.

I took Mabel to the finals two months later and we went into the dressing rooms to see Steve before his bout.

'Well,' I said, 'are you going to win it?'

He grinned at me and pointing to the scar tissue above his right eye he said, 'Aye, as long as this holds up.'

He won easily and in 1956 he was boxing professionally and Mabel and I watched him win again on television.

32

The Closure and the Scour

Big Bertha had done everything as Sandy predicted, an excellent job, which had speeded up the whole contract considerably, but she had been retired for almost a month, because the narrowing of the gap between the east and west ends had now produced a fearsome scour, that left no sand whatsoever on top of the sandstone bottom. This made the bottom waling more than seventeen feet above us, when we stood on the bottom. The scour was so powerful we could only dive for a period of two hours either side of the full and ebb tides. Any longer and we would be swept either into the bay or out to sea.

At eight o'clock one morning we arrived to find the offices deserted, not even the irascible Frank was behind the open hatch of the time office. From further down the site there came the sounds of revelry: voices raised in song accompanied by the obvious stamping of feet. Sandy and I looked at each other with puzzled amazement.

'What the hell is going on here do you think?' I asked, as we and our boat crew set off in the direction of the main canteen.

'Sounds like a celebration,' Sandy answered.

'Sounds like somebody's getting murdered,' said Billie.

Dod just grunted. 'Huh, sounds like a bunch of drunks to me.'

Buncer threw his oar in. 'I think Sandy's right and one hell of a party's going on.'

The noise increased as we neared the canteen and looking through the windows, we saw the complete night shift, labourers, piling crews and foremen, derrick drivers and dozer drivers, dump truck men and the Overseas Divers along with Matchet and Eric, and even Frank, *Frank with a smile on his face*. In the centre of the canteen stood a full-sized beer barrel, from which all the men were continually filling ordinary mugs and swallowing the beer as if their lives depended on it. They must have started their celebration some time ago, for everyone was well and truly drunk, except Eric, who looked completely out of place among them, but still tried a weak smile as he watched their drunken antics from an obviously stone-cold sober mind. At one table at the back of the canteen sat the Rameses twins, fair haired on the left, dark haired on the right. Their faces were as impassive as the Egyptian pharaoh I had likened them to. Each of their right hands rested on a mug of beer, which they neither drew towards them nor rejected. This was the first time I had seen them out of diving suits, since I had been called upon to clear the waling they had mangled months before. Jack Sayers and Tony Sparrow were there. They were the two men who would form the Company of North Sea Divers in the years to come and make their fortune. Also present was big Geoff Kane, the one man who caused Al Matchet to think again as regards interfering with underwater work.

Sandy had taken one look and walked away towards the job and now Buncer drew my attention away from the windows.

'Bobby, Sandy's shouting something to you.'

I saw the big fellow waving his arms about wildly and motioning us to hurry and join him. Normally placid in nature, it had to be something out of the ordinary to get Sandy worked up like this, so I broke into a run to join him. Closing the distance between us I could now hear him shouting.

'The stupid bastards have driven every pile of the closure, both inner and outer, with no way for the tide to get in to the bay!'

I pulled up beside Sandy and found myself looking at the meeting of the two ends. Before me were thirty-six freshly driven piles with no infill of red blaize between them.

'What's the problem Sandy?' I asked, for at this time in my diving career I had been more used with diving in the open sea all the time, whereas Sandy had more experience of dock work, lock gates, dry docks and sluice valves.

'They've driven every pile to its full set at the bottom of a spring tide, when they should have left every third one tack-welded above the high water mark to let the incoming tide into the bay.'

I immediately thought of the other coffer dams I had worked on at Portobello and the Forth Road Bridge and remembered the piles we used to leave up to allow the sea into them to equalise the pressure.

'What can we do Sandy, to stop the lot from being swept away?' I asked.

'We'll have to get every set of burning gear on the job and cut large hatches through the piles to let the water in, that might save it and it might not.' The look on Sandy's face told me he feared the effort would be in vain.

I may have been the chief diver on the job, but I was glad my big mate took over. He lit a fire under everyone's bottom and I witnessed the astonishing speed with which he galvanised the whole of the day shift labour force into action. The two derrick drivers quickly hooked on the man-help cages and swung them out over the water, containing men who could burn, and burning gear. Sandy meanwhile was giving some

241

men a crash course on burning, men who had never handled a torch in their lives. They were to slide down the inclined face of the fill and cut hatches immediately above the low tide mark. Sandy used yellow keel markers to roughly draw three-foot by one-foot hatches on the inside faces of the piles. Dod was burning away while wearing an open-necked shirt and got a blowback, which caused a globule of molten metal to hit him just below his windpipe. He snatched the shirt neck away from his skin, causing the globule to drop down inside his clothes and severely burned his manhood. His wife Eileen would later tell me she thought Dod should leave such a dangerous job.

Sandy leaned over the inner piles and shouted down to the Overseas Divers' boat below him, telling them to move away further inshore. The men on board ignored him and stayed where they were. The *Eadie* was moored outside the outer piles and Sandy roared at them as well to clear out of the danger area.

They needed no second telling and off they went, heading for the old harbour as fast as they could go.

I was burning my second hatch, when I was called up to speak to Eric who had arrived on the scene. In his normal quiet tone he asked, 'What is all this about Bobby? Mr Matchet deliberately drove the piles at low water to exclude as much water as possible from the bay, to save pumping out later.'

'Eric,' I replied, 'both Sandy and I agree, if we don't let the water into the bay the whole lot is liable to carry away.'

'Everything's standing fine at the moment,' Eric observed.

'Yes I agree, but there's at least sixteen or seventeen feet of water to come, since this will be one of the biggest spring tides of the year.'

Eric shook his head saying, 'You really believe it might sweep away the whole lot?' His eyes held an unbelieving look as he slowly shook his head again. 'It does appear to be standing fine,' he repeated.

I made a wide sweep with one arm as I said, 'Eric, this is a huge area of a bay and both Sandy and myself are not sure if we can save the job, even with all the hatches we're cutting out at the moment, but we just have to give it a try.'

Eric was silent for a few minutes, then asked, 'What happens to the holes if it does stand up?'

I now had to think pretty quickly but the answer was really self-evident.

'At low water again, we will have to weld plates over the lowest of them and fill up to their level with blaize, then same again the next low water.'

I could hear Sandy shouting at the Overseas boat again, telling them they were in danger lying where they were and to get to hell out of there, but once more the men on board ignored him. They sat on their deck housing and looked up at the first of the sea water dribbling through the bottom hatches as the tide started to make once more. I left Eric standing there watching us and jumped back on my cage. I was then swung out to the hatch I had been cutting and carried on with my job. An hour later Eric called us all up out of the area as the inner piles took a sudden lean shorewards. The sudden surge coincided with the lower hatches increasing their flow dramatically and jetting out more than twenty feet and thoroughly dousing the men in the Overseas boat. They had paid no attention to Sandy's warning and it was with a smile on my face that I watched them desperately trying to start their engine and get out of there. I suggested it might be a good idea to move the dozers and derricks back a good distance, just in case everything did carry away, and this was done. By this time most of the hatches were roaring like small Niagara Falls and a huge build-up of foam lay beneath them.

Both sets of piles then took another violent lean inwards and we thought they must surely carry away. The roar of water through the hatches increased and actually caused a vibration through the consolidated fill, all the way back to where we stood.

Even at some considerable distance away from the closure, we were still prepared for instant flight if she should go. The hours rolled by and the bay slowly filled, taking the head of water down to an acceptable level. There was no further change in the angle of the piles until the tide turned.

Eric had asked if we were willing to remain beyond the normal twelve-hour shift and we all agreed. Now we had the same problem, only in reverse, and we watched the piles straighten up and then begin to lean towards the seaward side. At low water we had the boat back and I dressed, went down and welded the lower plates and we filled up to them with blaize. The danger was over and we completed the fill, and the bulldozers firmed everything up. We never set eyes on Al Matchet after the day of the party and when I asked Eric about him, he told me he had been called away to another job.

So ended the Cockenzie job and of course, Sandy's diving career. I would be fully three years away from the underwater work and this was the time my wife Mabel miscarried the wee boy. I then resumed full-time diving work and Mabel gave birth to our last two daughters, Rosslyn and Pamela. I would continue diving for a further eleven years, despite some hair-raising experiences, but that must remain to be told later, in my second book, *Hard Hats 2*.

Hard Hats 2

Hard Hats 2 continues the author's diving experiences with the Leith Docks Commission and Forth Ports Authority. Sometimes humorous, as he describes the laughable incidents that took place during everyday diving, and sometimes tragic, as he recounts the lives lost accidentally or deliberately through either mishap or the sheer desperation of the troubled human soul.

He gives us a glimpse into a bygone age, before the advent of change altered life as it once was, in our diving practices, our harbours, our ships and the people who ran them.

A truly remarkable story.

Captain Douglas Watt